D1127281

The 1960s

War Within a War: Vietnam and the Cold War

Other titles in the Lucent Library of Historical Eras, The 1960s, include:

Arts and Entertainment
The Great Society: The War on Poverty
Life on the Front Lines: The Fight for Civil Rights

The 1960s

War Within a War: Vietnam and the Cold War

Laurel Corona

San Diego • Detroit • New York • San Francisco • Cleveland • New Haven, Conn. • Waterville, Maine • London • Munich

For more information, contact
Lucent Books
27500 Drake Rd.
Farmington Hills, MI 48331-3535
Or you can visit our Internet site at http://www.gale.com

LIBRARY OF CONGRESS CATALOGING-IN-PUBLICATION DATA

Corona, Laurel, 1949–
War within a war: Vietnam and the Cold War / by Laurel Corona.
p. cm. — (The Lucent library of historical eras. The 1960's)
Includes bibliographical references and index.
ISBN 1-59018-389-4 (hardback : alk. paper)
1. Vietnamese Conflict, 1961–1975—Juvenile literature. 2. Vitnamese Conflict, 1961–1975—United States—Juvenile literature. 3. United States—Foreign relations—1945–1989—Juvenile literature. 4. Cold War—Juvenile literature. [1. Vitnamese Conflict, 1961–1975. 2. Cold War.] I. Title. II. Series: Lucent library of historical eras. 1960's.
DS557.7.C67 2004
959.704'3—dc22

2003015981

Printed in the United States of America

Contents

Foreword

Looking back from the vantage point of the present, history can be viewed as a myriad of intertwining roads paved by human events. Some paths stand out—broad highways whose mileposts, even from a distance of centuries, are clear. The events that propelled the rise to power of Germany's Third Reich, its role in World War II, and its eventual demise, for example, are well defined and documented.

Other roads are less distinct, their route sometimes hidden from view. Modern legislatures may have developed from old tribal councils, for example, but the links between them are indistinct in places, open to discussion and interpretation.

The architecture of civilization—law, religion, art, science, and government—as well as the more everyday aspects of our culture—what we eat, what we wear—all developed along the historical roads and byways. In that progression can be traced every facet of modern life.

A broad look back along these roads reveals that many paths—though of vastly different character—seem to converge at a few critical junctions. These intersections are those great historical eras that echo over the long, steady course of human history, extending beyond the past and into the present.

These epic periods of time are the focus of Lucent's Library of Historical Eras. They shine through the mists of history like beacons, illuminated by a burst of creativity that propels events forward—so bright that we, from thousands of years away, can clearly see the chain of events leading to the present.

Each Lucent Library of Historical Eras consists of a set of books that highlight various aspects of these major eras. For example, the Elizabethan England library features volumes on Queen Elizabeth I and her court, Elizabethan theater, the great playwrights, and everyday life in Elizabethan London.

The mini-library approach allows for the division of each era into its most significant and most interesting parts and the exploration of those parts in depth. Also, social and cultural trends as well as illustrative documents and eyewitness accounts can be prominently featured in individual volumes.

Lucent's Library of Historical Eras presents a wealth of information to young readers. The lively narrative, fully documented primary and secondary source quotations, maps, photographs, sidebars, and annotated bibliographies serve as launching points for class discussion and further research.

In studying the great historical eras, students also develop a better understanding of our own times. What we learn from the past and how we apply it in the present may shape the future and may determine whether our era will be a guiding light to those traveling future roads.

Introduction: Flawed Vision, Fatal Path

There was a time when a map showing the red of communism spreading like spilled paint over the world could strike genuine fear in the hearts of Americans. There was a time when Americans believed that the Soviet Union would stop at nothing, including nuclear war, to destroy democracy. A mean-spirited Communist leadership had set its sights on suppressing freedom and pleasure everywhere, in favor of a drab world of anonymity, uniformity, and drudgery—or so Americans were told and believed.

Thus it was with great relief that the American people put their faith in leaders who promised that such a fate would not befall them. To the five Vietnam Era presidents, Harry Truman through Richard Nixon, and those who advised them, the way to ensure they could deliver on this promise was to stop the further spread of communism anywhere in the world. The pledge of an earlier president, Woodrow Wilson, that the United States would strive to "make the world safe for democracy"[1] after World War I was echoed after World War II by Dwight D. Eisenhower's "domino theory." This theory, which became the guiding ideology behind U.S. Cold War politics, held that if one country became Communist, its neighbors would as well, and their neighbors after them.

Ultimately, it was believed, communism would arrive on America's doorstep unless the United States marched out to meet and defeat it on the other side of the world. Only in that way could democracy and the American way of life be safeguarded. President John F. Kennedy alluded to the same goal in his inaugural address when he said that the United States would "pay any price, bear any burden, meet any hardship, support any friend, oppose any foe, to assure the survival and the success of liberty."[2] This commitment to "the survival and the success of liberty" entangled the United States in a long and devastating conflict in Vietnam. Vietnam, as American leaders saw it, was a place on a map that was not going to be painted red, a domino that was not going to fall.

A Conflict of Visions

It is clear today that the narrow Cold War focus of American leaders on defending against a Communist menace caused them to misunderstand the motivations of the Vietnamese, and unnecessarily extend what had already been a tragic chapter in history. While the United States perceived itself as involved in a Cold War conflict to prevent Communist expansion in Vietnam, the Vietnamese did not perceive the war that way at all. It is true that the country's primary political figure, Ho Chi Minh, openly spoke of his vision of a Communist future for all Vietnam. However, the typical Vietnamese soldier who lay in wait to ambush American military patrols, or who opened fire on American troops as they jumped from helicopters into remote villages, did so not because he or she wanted a Communist future specifically, but simply a united Vietnamese one, and one free of American control.

Instead of seeing a legitimate fight for the integrity of Vietnam as a nation, the United States was blinded by a vision of

In his 1961 inaugural address, President John F. Kennedy declared that the United States would "oppose any foe, to assure the survival and the success of liberty."

the Soviet Union pulling the strings of leaders, like North Vietnamese revolutionary Ho Chi Minh, all over the Communist world. But Ho, though an ardent Communist, was not the type to let any foreigner have power over him or his country. Putting Vietnam first also caused Ho often to be at odds with both Soviet and Chinese Communists, who had shown a willingness to betray Vietnamese interests when they did not match their own.

The war Ho led was not between north and south, or even primarily between Communists and non-Communists, but between those who would allow foreigners to dictate their future and those who would not. In the words of historian Marilyn B. Young, "What was so difficult for [Americans] to understand, although hundreds of prisoners, defectors and suspects said so in thousands of pages of transcript interviews, was that [Ho's supporters] . . . interpreted the support they received . . . as affirmation that Vietnam was one country."[3] This is a major reason why Ho achieved such heroic proportions in all of Vietnam and why in the end, his vision of a unified country could not be defeated even by the full military might of the United States.

A Terrible Toll

Still, the United States continued to listen to South Vietnam's constant calls for more money, more troops, more of everything, always justified by the fight against communism. As historian Robert Mann explains, American leaders "wrongly assumed that the war was primarily a military, not a political struggle,"[4] and thus their strategy relied on military strength alone. The U.S. inability to win outright victory, the skyrocketing number of Americans dead and wounded in battle, and the pictures of suffering Vietnamese on the nightly television news led many to believe that the war had no purpose legit-

Ho Chi Minh and his supporters envisioned a united Vietnam free of foreign control.

imate enough to justify such suffering. The absurdity of the American position was probably best summarized by one American officer who, on viewing the rubble left behind in one city after a bombing raid, said "we had to destroy the town in order to save it."[5]

Over years, dissent and divisiveness grew within the United States, eventually leading President Richard Nixon to seek "peace with honor" in Vietnam. As the last American combat troops left Vietnamese soil in 1973, the toll on American lives could be given some degree of finality. From 1961 to 1973, approximately 2,594,000 American soldiers served in Vietnam, and another million served elsewhere in Southeast Asia. Of these, 58,209 died, 47,343 in combat. Another 313,616 were wounded. It was the third-most-catastrophic war in U.S. history in terms of casualties, ranking after only the Civil War and World War II. As for casualties among the enemy, they are estimated to be many times higher, though numbers vary. Civilian casualties in the north were even higher. One source estimates 165,000 civilians were killed every year of Nixon's presidency alone, and several million died overall.

An Ongoing Reassessment

Today the war in Vietnam is still one of the most painful and difficult chapters in American history. Though opinions about what the United States should have done vary widely, the aftermath of the American withdrawal and the end of the Cold War are now facts. Vietnam was indeed reunified under Communist rule in 1975, although Ho, who died in 1969, did not live to see it. Neighboring Laos and Cambodia, in addition to Vietnam, have Communist governments today. No further dominoes fell, however, and eventually the Communist threat subsided with the fall of the Soviet Union.

The flaws in the domino theory are clear today, but then the threat seemed very real indeed. With hindsight, it now seems more accurate to summarize the role of Vietnam in the Cold War by saying simply that the Southeast Asian nation of Vietnam, as a result of the interests of several foreign nations over more than a century, had lost its ability to act independently. Like many other colonial nations, it wanted to take advantage of the political upheaval after World War II to become independent again. However, this desire was undermined by the emergence of the Cold War. The United States enforced an artificial division of the country to keep a strategic anti-Communist toehold in Southeast Asia, but the U.S. will to maintain this division by force was not as strong as the will of the Vietnamese people to resist.

If the United States had been able to see kinship between its own struggle for independence two hundred years earlier and that of the Vietnamese people to be free of those they considered oppressors, it might have cast itself in a different and more supportive role. It is easy today to look at the billions of dollars spent and millions of lives lost and envision how much good could have come from using lives and money differently. As an effort to promote democracy, the Vietnam War was unquestionably a failure. However, a different kind of victory can come from defeat when the lessons learned are substantial.

The Vietnam War seemed to lay to rest the idea that American military might was enough to shape another country's destiny. Added to this was the lesson that the United States was defeated at least in part because it did not treat the Vietnamese people, history, or culture with sufficient respect and because the United States could not distinguish its own perceived best interests from those of other people in other places. These are lessons the American Revolution taught the British, and values the American people gave the world. For Vietnam's legacy to be transformed into a positive one, these are lessons the American people and their leaders must continue to heed.

Chapter 1

The Cold War Comes to Southeast Asia

On September 2, 1945, World War II came to an end, when U.S. general Douglas MacArthur accepted the surrender of Japan on the USS *Missouri* as it lay at anchor in Tokyo Bay. One bloody chapter in American history was over. Thousands of miles away, another historic event was occurring, one that would shape the second half of the twentieth century as much as the two world wars had shaped the first. On the same day, in Ba Dinh Square in downtown Hanoi, the acknowledged leader of the Vietnamese people, Ho Chi Minh, stood in the bright sunlight and declared the independence of Vietnam from colonial rule.

He began his speech with words more familiar to the beaming, uniformed American officers in the audience than to the thousands of cheering Vietnamese. "All men are created equal. They are endowed by their creator with certain inalienable rights, and among these are life, liberty, and the pursuit of happiness."[6] This quotation from the American Declaration of Independence showed clearly Ho's admiration for the ideals of the United States and his desire for American support as Vietnam established itself as an independent nation. As he finished his speech, an American plane flew overhead, to wild applause. Within a few years, however, the smiles were gone. By the time two decades had passed, the sound of American planes overhead would herald only destruction and death.

Colonialism and French Indochina

To understand how such a promising start went so seriously wrong, it is important to understand just what Ho Chi Minh was declaring independence from. For eighty years, Vietnam had been ruled by France. In his independence day speech, Ho reminded the crowd of the legacy of French rule. "They have deprived our people of every democratic liberty. . . . They have built more prisons than schools. They have mercilessly slain our patriots; they have drowned our uprisings in rivers of blood. . . . They have robbed us of our rice fields, our mines, our forests and our raw materials." Furthermore, Ho went on, they had artificially divided one nation into three—Tonkin, Annan, and Cochinchina—"in order to wreck our national unity and prevent our people from being united."[7]

Ho Chi Minh meets with French leaders. The French controlled Vietnam until Ho declared the nation's independence in 1945.

The United States, partly because of its own history of fighting off colonial rule was a strong advocate for the end of colonial rule in Vietnam and elsewhere. President Franklin D. Roosevelt had particularly harsh feelings toward the French as colonial overlords in Southeast Asia, which the French called Indochina, and was as a result very supportive of the idea of a newly independent Vietnam. "France has milked [Indochina] for one hundred years. The people . . . are entitled to something better than that,"[8] he once remarked. French rule in Indochina had been briefly toppled by the occupying Japanese army during World War II, and Roosevelt was determined not to permit the French to reestablish themselves as colonial rulers after Japan's defeat and withdrawal. Even before the end of World War II, in April 1945, Roosevelt had sent an operative in the Office of Strategic Services (OSS), precursor to the Central Intelligence Agency (CIA), to lay the groundwork for covert operations to undermine any French attempt to reclaim Indochina when the

Communism

The Cold War was based on a conflict between two competing political and economic philosophies—communism and capitalism. The United States and the countries of Western Europe were built on the political philosophy of democracy and the economic philosophy of capitalism, or free enterprise. The Soviet Union and China followed the political and economic philosophy of communism. Communists believe that when people have personal rather than community gain as their goal, individuals will succeed only at the expense of others. Over time a class structure evolves in which most people stay poor but a small group becomes very wealthy. Such was the case in Vietnam, where peasants worked hard but lived in poverty, while the profits of their work went to their landlords.

Communists believed that if the workers collectively owned land or a factory, they could work it together and share the profits of their labor fairly among themselves. Their quality of life would improve because they would not be wasting profits on any owners. No one would be rich or poor, or have to worry about being housed, clothed, or fed. This idea had immense appeal in many countries. For years, the Vietnamese had seen the natural resources of their country drained and their own labor used to benefit foreigners and the rich upper class. Ho Chi Minh proposed the idea that land and other resources be taken from the rich and redistributed to the peasants. Many Vietnamese saw this as a solution to their problems. Ho was thus able to rally many Vietnamese around a vision of the future that contrasted greatly with the reality they faced under foreign rule.

Japanese were forced to withdraw by an Allied victory.

This officer, Major Archimedes Patti, was approached soon after his arrival in Vietnam by operatives of a military group known as the Vietminh. The Vietminh had been organized by Ho Chi Minh to fight back against foreign control, and by 1945, it was a small army of approximately three thousand members living and training secretly. Though Ho Chi Minh would later become the symbol of the evil of communism in Southeast Asia, at the time he seemed like America's best hope for a free Vietnam. Though he was an admitted Communist with the goal of establishing a nation along Communist lines, he was first and foremost a nationalist who hated foreign domination and thus would be unlikely to allow either the Soviet Union or China to gain a foothold in Vietnam. In fact, Ho's relationship with the leadership of the international Communist Party, the Comintern, had been a rocky and volatile one over this very issue.

Ho was already known to be interested in friendship with the United States. In fact, he had been trying to forge links with the United States in World War II as early as 1941. According to historian Loren Baritz, Ho had "once offered to guide a downed American pilot to safety, and . . . he was rewarded by an appointment to the OSS as Agent #19, code name Lucius, with the task of reporting Japanese troop movements to Washington."[9] The OSS responded to Ho's efforts by parachuting thousands of weapons to the Vietminh to use against the Japanese. Thus, though Ho was viewed by the United States as someone whose ideas might cause trouble in the long run, he was perceived as enough of an independent thinker, admirer of American ideals, and man of action to deserve support in the immediate postwar transition toward an independent Vietnam.

Conflicting Alliances

The United States, at the time of Major Patti's mission, was actually not paying much attention to Vietnam. President Roosevelt suddenly died and was succeeded by Vice President Harry S. Truman. Simultaneously, the United States dropped atomic bombs on Japan and brought World War II to a quick and stunning end. It was becoming increasingly clear that the global situation after the war would be tense as a result of Soviet leader Joseph Stalin's clear intentions to bring as much of Europe as possible into the orbit of the Soviet Union. Throughout its history, America's strongest relationships have been with the countries of Western Europe, with which it shares values, culture, and political systems. Thus, though building the nation of Vietnam was the center of Ho's world, it barely registered in the thinking of the Truman administration, which had as its top priority protecting its European allies by stopping the westward spread of communism across Europe.

The sudden change of American presidents and the equally sudden end to World War II affected global politics considerably. In fact, it was the unexpectedly quick defeat of the Japanese that led Ho to believe that the time was right to declare independence. Ho feared that the French would move back into his country and would simply pick up where they had left off before the war. Indeed, French president Charles de Gaulle had already declared France's intentions to restore their rule in Indochina, so Ho had reason to be worried about the French. He immediately sent a series of letters to President Truman, asking for his support against a resumption of French colonial rule; but rather surprisingly, given American interest at Vietnam's announcement of independence, all these letters went unanswered.

The problem, as the Truman administration saw it, was that France would be important in preventing Stalin from controlling more of Europe. France was vulnerable: It had been humiliated by Nazi occupation during World War II, and recovery of both its economy and its global prestige hinged on reestablishing itself as a major world power. Being forced to relinquish its colonies would therefore not help this process. Thus, the United States felt that support of its longtime ally France was both the diplomatic thing to do and the best means possible for protecting Western Europe from communism. This goal was seen as far more significant than helping the independence movement of an obscure country halfway around the world.

Ho's Efforts at Diplomacy

Meanwhile in Vietnam, in keeping with the terms of the Potsdam Conference of the Allied Forces of World War II, the Chinese occupied northern Vietnam to supervise the retreat of Japanese forces after their surrender. While there, according to historian Loren Baritz, "The Chinese troops engaged primarily in robbing the country blind"[10] for about a year. In the southern region, after the British removed the Japanese, they turned control back over to France. France soon brought thirty-five thousand troops to Indochina and began a ruthless campaign to rid the region of Vietminh. Soon, the southern half of Vietnam was under French control. The

When French president Charles de Gaulle (pictured) declared his intent to restore French rule in Vietnam, Ho Chi Minh sought help from the United States.

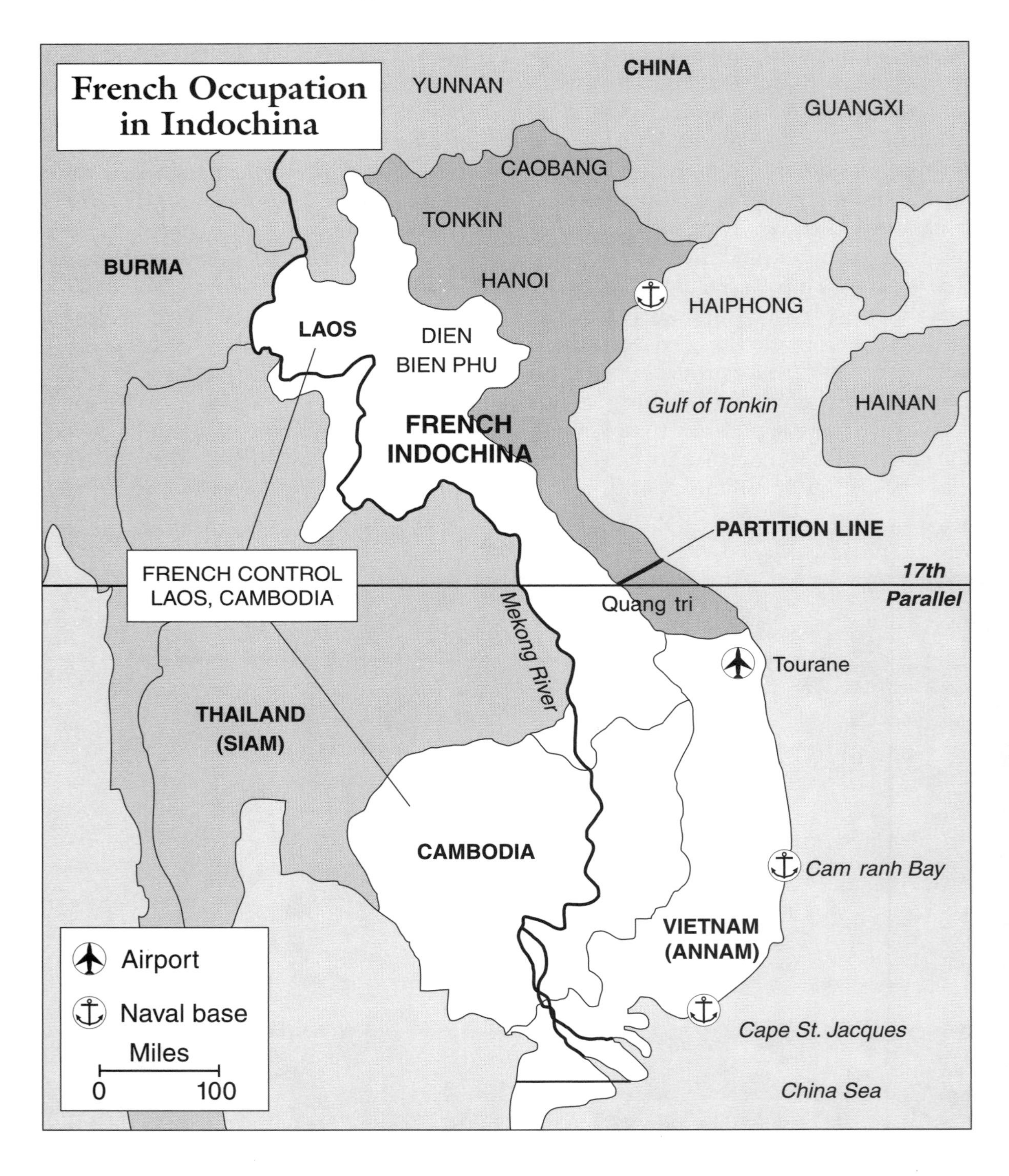
French Occupation in Indochina
YUNNAN
CHINA
GUANGXI
CAOBANG
TONKIN
BURMA
HANOI
HAIPHONG
LAOS
DIEN
BIEN PHU
Gulf of Tonkin
HAINAN
FRENCH
INDOCHINA
PARTITION LINE
FRENCH CONTROL
LAOS, CAMBODIA
17th
Parallel
Quang tri
Mekong River
Tourane
THAILAND
(SIAM)
CAMBODIA
Cam ranh Bay
VIETNAM
(ANNAM)
Airport
Naval base
Miles
0
100
Cape St. Jacques
China Sea

Ho Chi Minh and the Vietminh

Ho Chi Minh was one of the twentieth century's most influential leaders. His birth name was Nguyen That Thanh. He went by so many aliases, the best known of which was Ho Chi Minh, that many of his followers simply called him "the General." Ho was born in 1890 in central Vietnam. He got a job as a cook on a French ship and as a result ended up in London and Paris, living in both for many years. While there, he was exposed to the philosophy of communism and helped found the Communist Party of France. By the early 1930s, Ho had emerged as the leader of an early Communist-inspired group of Vietnamese fighting to end French rule. At one point Ho was arrested, but he managed to escape to Moscow. The Communist Party announced his death so as to protect him, and even held a memorial service, but in fact by 1938, Ho was in China planning a return to Vietnam.

By that point there had been several Communist-inspired uprisings in Vietnam against the French. French suppression of dissent was very harsh, which led only to greater hatred of their rule. For example, when the French ran out of handcuffs for prisoners they would piece together the heels and palms of prisoners with wire and immobilize them in what were known as "tiger cages." Seeking independence, Ho and other leaders met secretly in a cave in 1941, after the fall of France in World War II and the subsequent invasion of Vietnam by the Japanese. Sensing that the end of the war would give them a chance for independence, they formed the League for the Independence of Vietnam, known as the Vietminh. The Vietminh was not an army but a political group working to gain popular support for independence and a Communist state. When Vietnam was divided, the Vietminh became known as the National Liberation Front (NLF) in the south.

French then struck a deal with the Chinese whereby the French gave up colonial possession of a few ports in China in exchange for control of northern Vietnam. The deal was struck and the Chinese withdrew, leaving all of Vietnam once more in French hands.

Shocked at this further betrayal of Vietnamese hopes for independence, Ho Chi Minh nevertheless did not give up on working with the United States and its allies, or even with France directly. He agreed to allow France a limited military presence in all of Vietnam as a transitional phase toward independence provided that the French were gone by an agreed upon date a few years hence, that attacks against the Vietminh in the south stop immediately, and that France recognize the Republic of Vietnam as a nation and not as its colony. Eventually this agreement was modified to treat Vietnam as a free state within French Indochina. It was never completely clear what this meant, but Ho hoped to buy time to work out a diplomatic and peaceful path to independence.

Claiming that "it testifies to our intelligence that we should negotiate rather than fight,"[11] Ho continued to try every means at his disposal to make his position heard in the United States and with the other Western powers as well. As proof of the sincerity of his desires to put independence above Communist ideology, the Communist Party, at Ho's behest, dissolved itself in November 1945 and made other concessions to ensure that non-Communist voices would be heard in the new government. It was testimony to his great diplomatic skills and his unquestioned role as the leader of Vietnam that the people continued to accept what seemed like one defeat and humiliation after another, in the name of future independence and unification.

The French, however, quickly reneged on the agreement by announcing the formation of a separate Republic of Cochinchina in the south, a clear attempt to reestablish a smaller colony along the old lines. To add to the disappointment, the Truman administration continued to ignore Ho's letters of protest. Ho still held out hope that the United States might offer a way out of what looked to be the inevitability of war with France to secure independence. Ho even went so far as to propose to Truman that if Vietnam could not immediately reassert its independence from the French, it would accept the idea of being a trust territory administered by the United States while details of independence were worked out. Again, President Truman never replied.

Public statements by the Truman administration made it clear that the United States had no problem with France remaining in Vietnam as long as France seemed to be favorable, however vaguely, toward the country's eventual independence. This approach kept with the overall view at the time that securing Western Europe against communism was the most important consideration of American foreign policy. At the time, the consequences of losing the support of a man most of the world had not heard of, who lived in a country most people could not find on a map, seemed small indeed.

Ho and the Vietnamese people felt profoundly betrayed. The glorious independence day of the previous year seemed to have stood for nothing. Truman's failure to respond hardened Ho's feelings toward the United States. The question of who would govern Vietnam had pitted Ho against all those he had most hoped to have as allies. Diplomacy and accommodation were at an end. There was nothing to do at that point but try to undermine the French and wait for further developments that might lead to another bid for independence.

Bao Dai and the State of Vietnam

When a bloody month-long skirmish broke out in late 1946 over whether the French or the Vietnamese had the right to collect taxes in Haiphong harbor, it was finally put down by French military force, and the Vietminh Liberation Army (VMLA) went into hiding in the countryside. From there, Ho broadcast a radio message exhorting all Vietnamese to take part in a "war of national liberation."[12] For several years this war took the form of sabotage and quick attacks on French positions in a style of war known as guerrilla warfare. The French claimed to be in control of Vietnam, although they maintained this control only by military force.

The effort to remain in power in Vietnam was an expensive drain on France's

In 1946 Bao Dai (right) became leader of the State of Vietnam, one of three countries that comprised the French Overseas Union.

resources, and the French looked to the United States for military and financial assistance. Realizing America's strong Cold War concerns about the spread of communism, the French played down their desire to keep their colony and began to stress that they were there to fight communism. The existence of Communist China on Vietnam's northern border gave urgency to French claims that their efforts were holding off an invasion. They claimed their reason for being there was not to have Vietnam for themselves but to unite it under one non-Communist ruler.

The French declared that henceforth Vietnam would be known as the State of Vietnam (SOV), one of three states within what would be called the French Overseas Union. Cambodia and Laos were the other two states. The SOV's leader was to be Bao Dai, the former emperor who had been living in exile first in Hong Kong, then in Paris. When Bao Dai had been emperor before, he had never held any real power, but was an important symbol. The Vietnamese saw the emperor as having a "mandate from heaven" to rule, and though other forms of government might be in place, the emperor's existence was thought to be enough to give the Vietnamese people a sense of security and continuity. By bringing back Bao Dai and asking for world recognition of the SOV as a nation, the French hoped to cast Ho Chi Minh and his followers in the role of troublemakers with no legitimate cause.

When Bao Dai came to Vietnam from his home in France to take over as head of state, he quickly realized that the SOV was a sham. Historian Larry H. Addington describes the nature of this French concoction: "The French retained effective control over [Bao Dai's] army, his finances and his foreign policy, and his position as chief of state in Saigon turned out to be not much different from his old one as a powerless figurehead emperor in [the royal city of] Hue."[13] One eyewitness at the installation of Bao Dai as head of government commented that "the expressions on the faces of both the participants and the spectators gave one the impression that the whole thing was a rather poorly managed stage show, with the actors merely going through the motions."[14]

Bao Dai quickly returned in disgust to his villa on the French Riviera, but the French continued the charade with the prime minister, Nguyen Xuan. The French pressed Truman for diplomatic recognition of the Bao Dai government and the SOV, but he was reluctant because it was obviously not a government chosen by the Vietnamese people. Ho Chi Minh had won an election held shortly after the declaration of independence and so was still the only elected ruler of Vietnam. He had continued to fight to regain that power, and thus there was no legitimate way to recognize someone else.

Truman ended up endorsing the Bao Dai government in February 1950, despite the lack of justification, but not directly as a result of French pressure. The impetus came in August 1949, when the Soviet Union successfully tested its first

"Losing" China

In China, a two-decade-long civil war between the Communist forces of Mao Tse-tung and the forces of the ruling party, the Kuomintang, led by Chiang Kai-shek, began in 1927. Despite massive American aid to Chiang Kai-shek, Mao's army was able to push Kuomintang forces south until, by the end of 1949, they had been forced off the mainland altogether to the island of Taiwan. Mao then declared the establishment of the People's Republic of China, an event regarded as a tremendous disaster in the United States.

In the rhetoric of the Cold War, America had "lost" China. Using this term for something it had not owned or even directly controlled showed clearly the Cold War logic: Every nation had to choose a side for or against the "free world," exemplified by the United States. With Mao's victory, the two largest nations on Earth, the Soviet Union and China, were firmly under Communist control. The speed with which this had occurred left the United States wondering what country would be "lost" next.

The U.S. view was oversimplified. Different countries viewed communism in different ways, and they were not all in league with each other. In fact, Mao did not get along well with Soviet leaders at all, and their forms of communism were distinctly different. In Vietnam, Ho Chi Minh deeply mistrusted both China and the Soviet Union. American leaders did not understand that the philosophy of communism had natural appeal in countries ending a period of colonial exploitation. The perception that there was a sinister plan afoot to conquer the world was not an accurate way to interpret its spread.

nuclear bomb. Suddenly world communism became an even more threatening possibility. Within a few months of this nuclear test, the People's Republic of China and the Soviet Union, the two major Communist powers in the world, recognized Ho's Democratic Republic of Vietnam (DRV) as the legitimate government instead of Bao Dai's.

Despite the fact that covert efforts by U.S. intelligence services and studies by the State Department had consistently shown that Ho Chi Minh "was certainly a communist but . . . put nationalism first, had no known direct ties to the Soviet Union, was relentless in his pursuit of direct ties to the United States, and . . . was the strongest and perhaps the ablest figure in Indochina,"[15] the United States instead chose to support a Bao Dai–led Vietnam. A simple logic that was to pervade the entire Cold War began to emerge: If the Soviet Union and China supported something, it had to be bad. Because communism was evil, all actions undertaken by Communists had to be resisted. "Almost immediately," in the words of historian Larry H. Addington, "the Cold War mentality took over." [16]

The Truman Doctrine and the Containment of World Communism

Shaping foreign policy around the goal of containing the spread of communism is at the heart of the influential principle known as the Truman Doctrine. First spoken aloud in March 1947, the Truman Doctrine asserted that free people around the world looked to the United States for support when their freedom was threatened. It was thus the responsibility of the United States to come to their aid. That threat, the doctrine maintained, was communism. Communism spread not only by invasions of countries from the outside, but from what Truman called "internal aggression." When "armed minorities or . . . outside pressures" [17] were known to be conspiring to put Communist systems of government in place, it was America's obligation to help resist such pressures.

It was in that context that the Bao Dai government was recognized by the U.S. government. Shortly thereafter 10 million dollars was allocated to France to fight communism in Vietnam. However, it was not in Vietnam that the first fight against communism would be waged. In June 1950, within a few months of the recognition of the Bao Dai government, the Korean War broke out. For the next three years, until the fighting ceased in July 1953, Korea, and not Vietnam, served as a symbol of American resolve to fight communism.

Though the Cold War was focused on Korea, it also arrived in Vietnam with American recognition of the Bao Dai government. From that point forward, the United States began actively supporting the French in Vietnam, as a means of containing communism in Southeast Asia. Recognition of Bao Dai also stood once and for all as a rejection of Ho Chi Minh as the legitimate leader of the Vietnamese people. As a result, the United States made an enemy of a leader who had tried for years for the opposite result. Thus, the chain of events which would eventually lead America into a war in Vietnam was set in motion by this fateful decision.

The Grasshopper and the Elephant

"Wars start with political decisions, not combat."[18] This observation by historian Loren Baritz is illustrated by the experience of Vietnam. Long before American soldiers began dying in the jungles and rice paddies of Vietnam, a war intended to protect the world from communism was waged there with American money and other support. The 10 million dollars President Harry Truman gave the French in July 1950 was complemented that September by the arrival in Vietnam of a small group of American military advisers. Americans for the first time had set foot in Vietnam as part of a force set against Ho Chi Minh.

Over the course of the next few years, this advisory role grew, as did U.S. financial involvement. During the four years of what was called the Indochina War, historian David W. Levy reports that "almost eighty cents of every dollar being spent to fight the Vietminh was coming from the United States,"[19] a total of more than 3 billion dollars. This astronomical sum of money, particularly by 1950s standards, was only part of the total bill because the United States also directly supplied goods and services, such as transport planes with American service and flight crews, in addition to paying the costs of its advisory missions. American involvement in the Indochina War was mostly behind the scenes. If typical Americans were aware of their country's involvement at all, it was likely to have been only through brief news

French tanks roll toward Hanoi during the Indochina War. The United States contributed more than $3 billion to help the French regain control of Vietnam.

clips telling how their country was assisting the heroic French effort. The American public was largely indifferent to the details. Thus, without open scrutiny or debate, one political decision at a time, the United States inched closer and closer to combat.

A Growing Resistance

Ho Chi Minh once likened the struggle between the French and the Vietminh to a showdown between an elephant and a grasshopper. To defeat an elephant, a grasshopper must be very careful, very wily, and very patient. In Vietnam, Ho and his forces took their time, mounting sabotage and sneak attacks designed to demoralize the French into withdrawing. These attacks became bolder and more deadly when the new Communist People's Republic of China began supplying the VMLA with weapons and equipment it had captured during its own civil war in China. Not to be outdone by its Communist rival, the Soviet Union also began sending arms and other aid to the VMLA. Soon the VMLA was able to begin a campaign to regain territory rather than simply harass the French. For several years, control of patches of land shifted back and forth as the French forces and the VMLA fought each other.

The Vietnamese people, however, generally preferred peaceful life in their villages, even if peace meant French occupation. Though there was widespread support for Ho, there was less enthusiasm for an all-out war to get rid of the French. Furthermore, the Vietnamese people did not have a clear image of how a Communist-style government would benefit them, in part because they had not seen concrete evidence in their own lives of what Ho intended to achieve. It became clear to Ho, after protracted battles for small patches of land, that he was not likely to reach his goal of a united, independent Vietnam by that means alone because the people were not likely to rise up and fight for it. Ho's passionate Communist convictions led him to believe that if the Vietnamese people could glimpse a Communist future they would want it badly enough to struggle hard to achieve it.

Because French control of Vietnam was mostly limited to the cities, Ho and the newly reestablished Communist Party, the Lao Dong, concentrated on implementing Communist ideas in the countryside. They abolished unfair arrangements whereby peasants worked to exhaustion only to have most of the profits go to rich landlords. Land was taken from these landlords and redistributed to the peasants. These peasant farmers worked together in what were known as collectives to increase their crop yields, and they soon saw their living conditions improve. In this way, Ho was able to contrast what the French offered with what communism offered, and a commitment to him and to his ideas began to take hold among many peasants. In the words of author Marilyn B. Young, "In the midst of the bitter military struggle with France, indeed as an integral part of that struggle, [Ho] conducted an agrarian revolution that transformed the countryside. The twin goals of revolution and nationalism that had marked all of Ho Chi Minh's life were now entirely fused."[20]

France's Army

The growing support for Ho and the increased capabilities of the VMLA required a greater investment of troops and weapons by the French. However, at home in France, there was little enthusiasm for a continued war. Many French were supportive of at least the ideals of communism, and the French Communist Party was a significant enough political force in the country to make waging the war an uncomfortable undertaking for the French government. Many French also were beginning to feel that colonization was wrong, and they were not willing to send soldiers to die in an effort to maintain it. As a result, the French government could put no more than eighty thousand of their own troops in Vietnam without incurring severe public backlash. The French were badly outnumbered and no longer had superior arms to offset this fact. It would be essential to expand its army using the Vietnamese themselves.

The French army thus began enlisting Vietnamese and Laotian soldiers into the French forces, which were renamed the Vietnamese National Army (VNA). The VNA technically served the Bao Dai government, but it was under strict supervision of the French. The seventy-six thousand members of Bao Dai's army and the approximately two hundred thousand Indo-Chinese inductees into the French army were largely draftees who had been forced to serve. Additionally, many Catholics volunteered their services to Bao Dai. As a religious minority, comprising only around 20 percent of Vietnam's population, Catholics were worried about the place they would have in Ho's Vietnam. Despite Ho's generally widespread support among the Vietnamese people, many others, in addition to Catholics, were also willing to join the VNA to fight against Ho. This was rarely from any real convictions about the French cause, but because past history indicated that the colonial forces would probably prevail and it would be better to be on the winning side when they did.

The Ho Chi Minh Trail

What had begun as isolated skirmishes between armies whose total numbers were well below 100,000 had become, by the end of 1951, a conflict involving two well-equipped armies each numbering in excess of 350,000. To move VMLA troops, supplies, and arms within Vietnam, a network of roads and footpaths along the mountainous border between Vietnam and Laos, known as the Ho Chi Minh Trail, was established. With the establishment of the Ho Chi Minh Trail, attacks increased against French strongholds in southern Vietnam.

It was becoming increasingly clear to the French that the Ho Chi Minh Trail was a key element in the VMLA's war strategy. Raoul Salan, the general in charge of the French army forces in Vietnam, ordered bombings and armed patrols of key sites along the trail. However, this was not easy to do because the trail was largely hidden in dense foliage and was little wider than a human body along much of its length. Bomb damage was quickly repaired or detoured around, and French patrols were frequently ambushed and destroyed. The effectiveness of the VMLA in countering the best French efforts was a great morale builder for them and served to embolden the Vietminh in their attacks on the French armed forces.

By 1953, French strategy began to revolve around neutralizing the Ho Chi Minh Trail to prevent the VMLA from resupplying and regrouping at will. At the same time, the French government was beginning to discuss ways of getting out of Vietnam altogether. The exit, the French government and military agreed, had to come on the heels of a great French military victory. This would enable the French to dictate the terms of their withdrawal and thus save face as well as preserve some of their economic privileges in the region. Thus, a strategy was devised to

Nguyen Thi Dinh

Many of the most active fighters in Vietnam were women, comprising what was nicknamed "the long-haired army." Nguyen Thi Dinh was the most important southern woman in the Vietnam War. Born into a peasant family in Ben Tre, on the Mekong Delta, she fought with the Vietminh forces against the French in her teens and spent three years in jail from 1940 to 1943. She was a founding member of the National Liberation Front (NLF) in her province, and in 1960 she led an insurrection in Ben Tre against Ngo Dinh Diem's government. There, fewer than two hundred men and women, armed with homemade explosives and old rifles, made incursions on government outposts, armed themselves with captured weapons, and grew into a full-sized army company. Eventually they forced the withdrawal of the Army of the Republic of Vietnam (ARVN) from much of the province and returned to the peasants farmlands confiscated by the government.

In 1965 Nguyen Thi Dinh became chair of the South Vietnam Women's Liberation Association and was appointed deputy commander of the NLF, the highest-ranking combat position held by a woman. She was especially effective at mobilizing village women to be part of the effort to liberate South Vietnam. For example, when the South Vietnamese army occupied the village of Phuoc Hiep, soldiers executed twenty young men and buried them prominently in various spots around the village. Nguyen's group, five thousand strong from six different villages, poured into the village serving as district headquarters of the army, demanding that the army withdraw from Phuoc Hiep. For five days and nights they stayed in front of district headquarters singing revolutionary songs and encouraging ARVN soldiers to desert. The army backed down and withdrew from Phuoc Hiep. After the war ended, Nguyen Thi Dinh continued to be active within the Vietnamese Communist Party. Her memoir, *No Other Road to Take,* was published in 1976. She died in 1992.

Nguyen Thi Dinh spent most of her life fighting for an independent Vietnam.

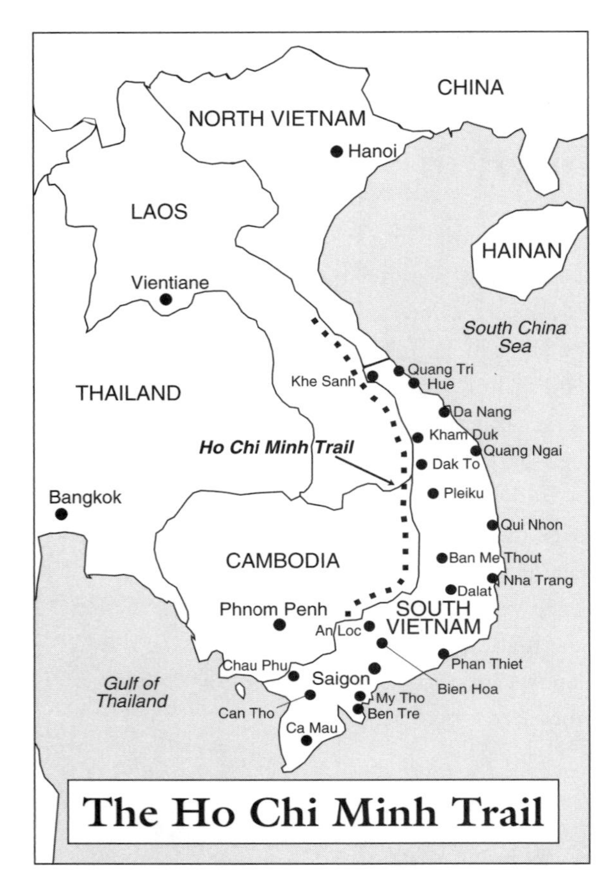

The Ho Chi Minh Trail

draw the VMLA into combat at a key point along the trail.

Dien Bien Phu

That strategic point was the village of Dien Bien Phu, on the Laos border in northwest Vietnam. The French had recently captured Dien Bien Phu and were using it to attack critical spots on the trail, to prevent supplies from China and the Soviet Union from reaching the south. General Henri Navarre was charged with beefing up French presence there specifically to provoke a reaction from the VMLA. The French installed approximately fifteen thousand troops, six bombers, and ten tanks and erected earthen barricades and towers to protect the soldiers and equipment. Navarre felt that the VMLA would have no choice but to commit huge numbers of soldiers to try to take Dien Bien Phu back, and that the losses they would incur as a result would give the French the upper hand again in the war.

Navarre and his soldiers waited for four months for the VMLA to attack. So impatient was Navarre that he ordered leaflets dropped on the surrounding villages taunting "What are you waiting for? Why don't you attack if you aren't cowards? We are waiting for you!"[21] What he did not know was that the VMLA was indeed waiting for something. In fact, one of the most remarkable human efforts in military history was in the making. A force of two hundred thousand Vietnamese—both civilians and soldiers, including women, men, and children alike—were in the process of carrying, mostly on foot, parts of two hundred weapons such as machine guns and small cannons called howitzers, along with tons of ammunition and other supplies, sometimes from hundreds of miles away. New trails had to be hacked through the jungle to assist in the moving of supplies and to get around the continual strafing and bombing of the trail by the French.

Four divisions of VMLA soldiers, forty-nine thousand in all, carried their own weapons and supplies, arriving in small groups to hidden locations just outside the French installations. According to Marilyn

B. Young, "Roped to the heaviest artillery pieces, men dragged the guns through the last fifty mile stretch of jungle, where no roads could be built. . . . When they reached the French base, they reassembled the heavy guns and set them up in caves dug deep into the hillsides so that they were invisible from the air."[22] While others were engaged in this backbreaking transport work, local people dug trenches and tunnels all the way to the edges of the French fort. The effort had taken the entire four months. In the estimation of Vietnamese general Vo Nguyen Giap, the head of the operation, if the number of participants were multiplied by the number of days each had worked, the project had taken 3 million workdays.

Questions remain today as to how aware the French were of this massive buildup. Apparently they knew of some of it, but as Loren Baritz explains, "the trouble was that the more accurate [French intelligence] was the less the military command believed it."[23] In keeping with Ho's analogy of the grasshopper and the elephant, it was impossible for the French to believe that the Vietnamese around Dien Bien Phu could be a true threat. It was inconceivable that the French could be outgunned, when it seemed clear that no heavy

The Vietminh defeat the French at Dien Bien Phu. The French made significant tactical blunders at the battle that resulted in their defeat.

artillery could be brought in except by plane, as the French had done.

In the end, however, the French were annihilated when the attack was finally launched on March 13, 1954. The first attack lasted only an hour, resulting in a massacre of several thousand French on the first day alone. Survivors expressed shock that the attack had begun in some cases from hidden locations only yards from their positions, and that their every move had evidently been watched and every location of weapons and ammunition was known in advance.

The French defeat was so quick and considered so disgraceful that the artillery commander committed suicide after the battle, using a hand grenade. Although the French fought back, inflicting by the end of the campaign as many as twenty thousand VMLA casualties, after a few days it was clear the French situation was hopeless. They were surrounded and trapped in the valley of Dien Bien Phu. Inability to fly or truck in supplies or remove the injured and dead because of hostile fire created a situation that French historian Bernard Fall described as "hell in a very small place."[24]

The Domino Theory

Facing the prospect of certain defeat at Dien Bien Phu, French chief of staff Paul Ely made a direct appeal to the Joint Chiefs of Staff of the American armed forces. The goal of containing the spread of communism was a major factor in American willingness to listen to Ely's appeal. President Dwight D. Eisenhower had recently coined the term "domino theory" to describe how a Communist victory in one place would lead to a victory in a neighboring place, until the whole world had fallen like a row of lined-up dominoes.

To prevent such a fall, some of Eisenhower's advisers were supportive of the idea of coming to France's aid, using bombers to attack VMLA positions. There was even some discussion of using small nuclear weapons. However, army chief of staff Matthew Ridgway pointed out that to secure more than an immediate victory at Dien Bien Phu would require a large commitment of ground troops. Unless the Americans were willing to back up this one strike with a continued presence, there was no point in getting involved. President Dwight D. Eisenhower faced a very clear dilemma. He did not want to be drawn into a war, especially so soon after the Korean War, which had ended just the year before. However, he had won the election on the promise to oppose Communist expansion strictly, and he did not want to allow the VMLA even one victory.

Eisenhower decided that the United States would consider rescuing the French at Dien Bien Phu, but only if it did not have to act alone. He found the British and other allies unwilling to participate because they felt France had in large part brought the situation on itself by attempting to hold onto its colonies by military force. Not as concerned as Eisenhower was about the consequences of the domino theory, they favored letting the French

French and Vietnamese prisoners that surrendered at Dien Bien Phu are led into captivity.

face defeat, after which a peace settlement could be negotiated at an international conference.

At home, Eisenhower also had recently received a lukewarm reaction to his first public unveiling of his domino theory at a press conference. This indifference led him to realize that the American public had not yet accepted the validity of the domino theory and was not convinced that a Communist Indochina represented any real eventual threat to the American way of life. He saw, from public indifference to the potential fall of Indochina, that not intervening would have no political fallout for him because it would not be perceived as softness on communism. In the words of historian Larry H. Addington, "an American failure to prevent a French defeat in Vietnam [would not] be blamed on the administration and dim its luster."[25]

As a result of all these factors, Eisenhower told the French the United States would not offer them assistance at Dien Bien Phu. Eisenhower was still deeply convinced of the validity of the domino theory and passionately committed to containing the spread of communism, but he figured there must be other ways to accomplish this without drawing Americans directly into the line of fire, or hinging his reputation as president on the rescue of a dying colonial power.

The Geneva Accords

On May 6, 1954, the French surrendered at Dien Bien Phu. The grasshopper had indeed brought down the elephant. The Vietnamese felt that surely this would mark the successful end of their battle for independence. However indifferent the Western powers may have been to the French position at Dien Bien Phu, they were not indifferent to what happened afterwards, and the efforts of Ho Chi Minh to unify a free Vietnam were only to become more complicated after Dien Bien Phu. As Marilyn B. Young explains, the Geneva Conference, which after the fall of Dien Bien Phu turned its attention to developing a peace settlement, "reflected neither the aspirations of the Vietnamese nor the military and political victory of the Viet Minh, but rather the hard realities of Cold War power."[26]

The Geneva Accords, a product of this conference, were designed to promote a temporary solution to the situation in Vietnam in a manner that assured both Communist and Western powers of a balance in Southeast Asia between their competing interest—in other words, they thought it best if Vietnam were split in two. This suited everyone except the Vietnamese. The People's Republic of China, for example, was not particularly concerned whether all of Vietnam was Communist but wanted to be sure it had a like-minded state, even a small one, on its immediate border. China was worried that America's passionate statements about containing communism might lead it into greater involvement in Vietnam, and it did not want to share a border with a country dominated by the United States. According to Chinese historian Qiang Zhai, "Under the pressure of Beijing and Moscow, the Viet Minh had to abandon its effort to unify the whole of Vietnam."[27]

Thus, rather than winning the full victory he had hoped for, after several months of negotiations Ho was able to win only the concession that Vietnam would be temporarily divided into two military zones at the seventeenth parallel, roughly the center of the country, and that in two years' time, in July 1956, elections would be held that would reunify the country under the victor. In the south, the government of Bao Dai would temporarily continue as the SOV. Ho Chi Minh would be immediately recognized as the legitimate leader of the Democratic Republic of Vietnam (DRV) in the north. The French had to withdraw altogether before the elections. No foreign armies or bases would be permitted to operate anywhere in the country, nor could either the SOV or the DRV ally themselves with or accept military aid from any foreign country. During the two years leading up to the election, all Vietnamese citizens were free to move between the two parts of the country and settle wherever they wished.

The Invention of South Vietnam

The United States did not participate in or sign the accords. It only stated that it took

SEATO

President Eisenhower's secretary of state, John Foster Dulles, was one of the major forces behind the development of strategies to contain communism. He was instrumental in creating a new organization called the Southeast Asian Treaty Organization (SEATO) in 1954. It was meant to resemble the North Atlantic Treaty Organization (NATO), which bound the United States and its key European allies in a pact by which each agreed to come to the defense of any member under attack by any foreign power. However, only two of the eight SEATO signatories, Thailand and the Philippines, were actually in Southeast Asia. Other signatories included Great Britain, France, Australia, New Zealand, and Pakistan.

The American goal in proposing SEATO, however, was not really mutual assistance between members; in fact, the United States insisted on language that would not obligate it to assist member nations unless they were threatened in some way by communism. In the words of historian Larry H. Addington, in *America's War in Vietnam,* "The primary usefulness of SEATO to the United States was to give the United States a cloak of international authority to take military action on behalf of . . . Vietnam, Cambodia or Laos." The creation of SEATO gave the United States a means by which it could openly disregard the Geneva Accords, by asserting its right under SEATO to defend the interests of all Southeast Asia by fighting communism in Vietnam.

Secretary of State John Foster Dulles presides over a Southeast Asian Treaty Organization meeting in 1955.

note of them and would not disturb them unless there was a renewal of aggression in the region that required a U.S. response. It was extremely disappointed that Ho Chi Minh had gained international recognition as a leader and that he would thenceforth be in control of territory internationally recognized as legitimately under Communist control. Furthermore, without outside interference, in only two years Ho was

Bao Dai

Bao Dai was the last Vietnamese emperor. He was born Prince Nguyen Vinh Thuy, in the Hue province of Vietnam in 1913. At the age of twelve, while he was in boarding school in France, his father, Emperor Khai Din, died. After returning home to be crowned Emperor Bao Dai ("Keeper of Greatness"), he went back to France to complete his schooling. In part because of this early upbringing, Bao Dai developed a strong preference for life in France and showed no interest in actually living in Vietnam. Bao Dai lived a lavish lifestyle, complete with women, fast cars, and gambling. Living a wealthy life in France made him unable to see the problems of colonial rule at home. For Bao Dai, colonialism was working very well.

As a boarding-school student in France, Bao Dai began to develop an appreciation for French culture.

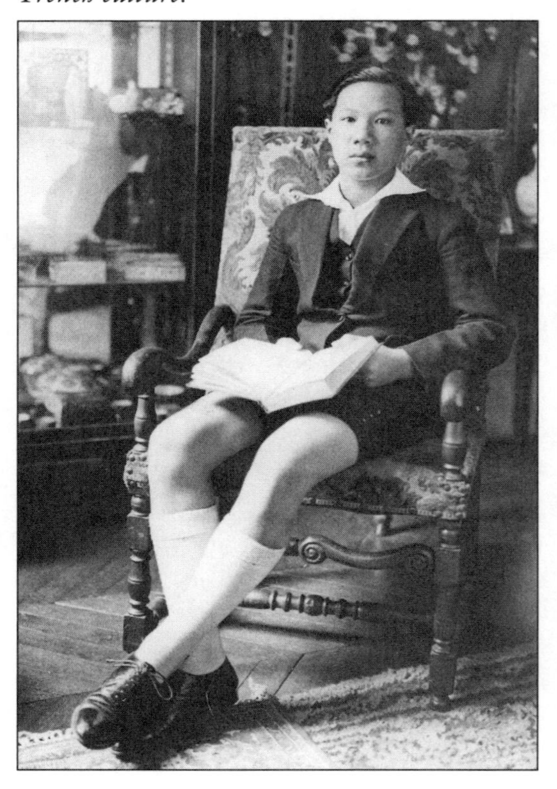

Bao Dai was willing to work with the Japanese occupiers as well as with the French, and this willingness to transfer his loyalty to another occupier rather than to take the initiative to use his power to assist those fighting for independence was what turned Ho Chi Minh decisively and permanently against him. After Japan was defeated in 1945, Bao Dai was forced to abdicate his throne, and he lived in exile until 1949 when the French government decided to reinstate him as head of the new State of Vietnam. After the Geneva Accords were in place, Bao Dai lost a popular referendum to Ngo Dinh Diem and subsequently left Vietnam for good. He retired to the French Riviera for a life of golf, bridge, and other pastimes. Bao Dai died on August 2, 1997, in a military hospital in Paris.

likely to win the nationwide elections and gain control of all Vietnam. The United States was not going to allow this to happen.

Almost from the minute the accords were signed, the United States began efforts to undermine them. The Eisenhower administration sent a small team of CIA agents to the DRV, under the direction of air force colonel Edward Lansdale, to weaken Ho's government by spreading lies and rumors and to sabotage public services to make the government look as if it could not function. Rumors about an imminent American attack with nuclear weapons sent nearly a million people fleeing from the north to the south by boat and on foot, a tricky publicity stunt designed to show that people were desperate to escape communism. Another campaign focused on Catholics, whose priests said outrageous things to their parishioners, including the claim that Jesus himself was waiting for them in the south with land and jobs. Marilyn B. Young points out that "the usefulness of this refugee population did not end with their much photographed arrival in the South. In effect they were an imported political resource . . . a substantial and dependent bloc of loyal supporters"[28] for the regime in the south.

The southern regime was now in the hands of a strongly pro-American premier, Ngo Dinh Diem. Bao Dai had been encouraged to name Ngo Dinh Diem as premier, a position which gave him responsibility for running the country, in return for which Bao Dai had been allowed to return to his life on the French Riviera. Immediately upon the appointment of Ngo, the United States announced, in flagrant disregard of the Geneva Accords, that it was providing Ngo with 2 billion dollars to make improvements in the SOV army. The United States claimed that these funds were to be used to make the transition from an army loyal to and trained by the French to one loyal to the SOV. They were also intended to enable Ngo to battle the growing trade in opium and other drugs and to fight armed and violent religious and other sects who were making the rule of law difficult to uphold in the south. All of these were real problems, but the American aid was really intended to help Ngo fight the Vietminh in the region south of the seventeenth parallel.

Ngo had no particular skills or talents, but because he could be counted on never to negotiate with Ho, he was in the American view a suitable choice to lead the SOV. However, it was obvious he would not win a fair and open election as required in 1956 by the Geneva Accords. "Almost any type of election would . . . give the Communists a very significant if not a decisive advantage,"[29] a secret State Department document advised Eisenhower. To ensure that a countrywide election did not occur, the United States developed a plan whereby the people in the south would have their own election between Bao Dai and Ngo Dinh Diem. The ballot would ask voters if they favored deposing the emperor in favor of naming Ngo chief of state for the purpose of imposing a democratic regime in southern Vietnam. Ngo won against the absentee emperor in a landslide. Indeed, the results were too good to be true. Despite the fact that there were 450,000 registered voters in Saigon, ballot-box stuffing and other fraudulent tactics gained Ngo more than 600,000 votes.

The Geneva Accords strictly prohibited the seventeenth parallel being viewed as a political boundary, but after this election, the permanent division of Vietnam was a foregone conclusion. Ho found that even his strongest allies, the Soviet Union and China, favored making a divided Vietnam permanent, since it would mean recognition of northern Vietnam as an independent Communist state by the other nations of the world and would be a clear gain for world communism. Completely isolated, Ho could only watch while Ngo followed his own rigged election with another equally corrupt one to choose a National Assembly for the south.

After these elections the United States announced that the Ngo government and the renamed Republic of Vietnam (ROV) had proven itself stable and democratic and therefore would enjoy official recognition by the United States. From that point forward, the ROV was known generally by the informal name South Vietnam, and the DRV was referred to as North Vietnam. Ngo managed to convince American leaders that dissent in the south was not caused by South Vietnamese citizens, but by northern infiltrators whom he called the Vietcong, who had sneaked into the country to undermine him. This gave rise to the American view that the problems with political stability in the south could be controlled by attacking and neutralizing the north. South Vietnam, the American government felt, had to be protected at all costs from the menace posed by the first Communist country in Southeast Asia.

Chapter 3

"By All Means Short of War"

Keeping the new Communist nation of North Vietnam from spreading its influence southward became a major foreign policy objective for the Truman, Eisenhower, and Kennedy administrations. To this end, Truman commissioned a secret report known as NSC-68. Prepared for the National Security Council, NSC-68 analyzed the overall situation in Southeast Asia and suggested possible strategies. The authors of the document were clear about the seriousness of the Communist menace in the region. "By all means short of war,"[30] the authors of NSC-68 argued, America needed to act to stop communism in its tracks.

Central in this strategy was supporting certain foreign leaders, even if they had little if any popular support or leadership skills. Indeed, leaders could be supported simply for being anti-Communist. One such leader was Ngo Dinh Diem. Over the nine years of Ngo's presidency, despite clear evidence that he ruled corruptly and cruelly, American money and other forms of support poured into South Vietnam.

Watching this new influx of American money and influence, Ho Chi Minh abandoned the idea of uniting Vietnam for the time being, focusing instead on implementing his vision of a Communist state in the north. To accomplish this, he established stronger links with both the Soviet Union and China, each of whom were eager to cooperate in order to maximize their own and minimize the other's influence in

Ho Chi Minh (right) meets with Chinese leader Mao Zedong in 1955. In an effort to establish a Communist state in North Vietnam, Ho solicited help from China and the Soviet Union.

Southeast Asia. Historian Qiang Zhai explains that "between 1955 and 1957, assistance from China and the Soviet Union played an important role in the DRV's efforts to reconstruct and develop its economy. Beijing and Moscow provided crucial raw materials, technical know-how and consumer products, helping lay a foundation for the later development of heavy industry in [North] Vietnam."[31] Thus for a while it appeared as if a peaceful coexistence between north and south might indeed be possible, but the truth was that Ho Chi Minh was simply biding his time to see what developed with the Ngo regime.

Oppression and Opposition

Despite his questionable "landslide" victory over Bao Dai, Ngo never had much popular support. He was an opportunist who had no real vision for Vietnam other than to use his power to promote his own family and friends. He put relatives in key positions regardless of their suitability, then did not hold them accountable if they bribed, tortured, or otherwise mistreated the citizenry. Ngo knew that what the United States feared most was communism. He correctly concluded that he would be able to use whatever tactics suited him to suppress the National Liberation Front (NLF, the resistance movement in

South Vietnam) as long as he claimed it was part of the fight against communism.

From the beginning, Ngo's regime was characterized by brutality and force. Immediately after his election, as a means of intimidating possible dissenters, he ordered arrest, imprisonment, and execution of thousands of NLF members. He ordered whole villages destroyed and entire families killed if they were suspected of supporting the opposition. He abolished the traditional local councils that governed villages and put his own administrators in their place. The NLF had been successful at driving many wealthy landlords off their lands and giving the land to the peasants to farm. Ngo required the peasants either to rent or purchase the land, which they could not afford to do. All of these things led to growing resentment of his regime.

The NLF took advantage of this discontent. They temporarily set aside their goal of establishing a Communist state in a united Vietnam in favor of developing the widest possible base of support for a campaign to get rid of Ngo. Because the United States automatically equated opposition to Ngo with support for communism, they continued to send Ngo whatever money and supplies he needed to suppress dissent.

Despite the fact that there were many reasons to oppose Ngo, all dissent was viewed by Americans as stemming from a single source—the Vietcong, an imprecise label slapped onto opposition forces by the United States. Soon American leaders began using this vague name seriously to describe the enemies of the Ngo regime. The term *Vietcong* was used by Americans as a synonym for Ho's supporters, whether in the north or south, army or civilian, but it actually included thousands who were united in opposition to Ngo but did not care about communism at all. Blurring the differences between his opponents by calling them all Vietcong, Ngo was able to convince the United States that every act of sabotage, every assassination of one of his

Ngo Dinh Diem ruled South Vietnam with brutality and force.

appointed village leaders, every revolt that had to be put down by his army was the work of the Vietcong and thus was supported, if not directly planned, by the Communist government in the north.

In this way Ngo was able to get the United States to commit more and more money to his regime. These funds were supposedly for increasing the size of his army, but much of the money was diverted to enhance the lifestyle and personal fortunes of Ngo and his associates. Additionally, the number of Americans in Vietnam as advisers, special operatives, and support staff continued to grow. Little by little U.S. direct involvement in Vietnam was increasing. Although there still were not any official combat troops in Vietnam, the number of military personnel had risen from 3,000 in 1961 to 11,500 in 1962.

Ho Chi Minh and the Purification Program

Despite the American perception that Ho Chi Minh was fomenting rebellion in the south, a more accurate picture was that the south was rebelling of its own accord. Ho, in fact, had his hands full trying to establish the nation of North Vietnam. He would have been justified in intervening diplomatically or even militarily to stop Ngo Dinh Diem's bid for power and force a true nationwide election as required by the Geneva Accords. Ho did not do this, largely because he thought such an effort would involve the United States more deeply in Vietnam and could result in a military occupation or a replay of the years of colonial rule.

Ho also knew that his chief allies, the Soviet Union and China, were satisfied with the arrangement and that he could not win militarily without their financial support. Instead, he tried to focus on what to him was the one positive thing about a divided Vietnam. For years Ho had tried to keep the focus first on liberating Vietnam from rule by outsiders, and only secondarily on achieving a Communist revolution. Now that a Communist state had been declared in North Vietnam, he no longer had to compromise. The time was right to build in North Vietnam the Communist state he hoped eventually would prevail in the whole country.

Ho and his small committee of about twenty advisers decided to move immediately to replace the old system of land ownership. They decided that the 2 percent of the people who were landlords must be held accountable for their exploitation of the peasants. The Communist Party, or Lao Dong, embarked on what was called a "purification program." Villages were charged with identifying anyone who had participated in oppression of peasants. The Lao Dong would rarely accept a village's claim that no one had been an enemy of the people, so villages were sometimes forced to please the Lao Dong by identifying neighbors as landlords, regardless of their actual experiences with them. In some cases, villages that would not falsely identify friends and family were forced to draw lots to decide who would be identified as a landlord. Those accused were tried, with the outcome almost always a

NSC-68

In 1950 President Truman asked the secretaries of state and defense to put together a study advising him how to protect America from communism. This document, known by its serial number, NSC-68, became a blueprint for American foreign policy from that point to the end of the Cold War.

The essence of NSC-68 was that keeping the Soviet Union from conquering more of the world was not sufficient to halt communism. It argued that the Soviet Union now pulled the strings of other countries such as China, getting them to fight for world Communist domination on Soviet behalf. It was not possible anymore to make a distinction between directly challenging the Soviet Union and more indirect and peripheral fights against Communist influence in remote countries all around the world. By this logic, helping Vietnam resist the influence of Ho Chi Minh was a vital American interest in its battle against Soviet world domination.

With nuclear weapons now in the arsenals of both sides, direct war was not an answer, although NSC-68 argued it would be necessary to begin a massive buildup of weaponry and new weapons capabilities in order to ensure that the Soviets did not outpace the United States. Additionally, the United States would have to work diligently to destroy communism where it already existed and to get newly emerging colonial powers to reject it. Sabotage, spying, psychological warfare, and other covert activities designed to foment rebellion within Communist countries were seen as appropriate ways to do this, as was direct military and other assistance to anti-Communist governments. Top secret at the time, NSC-68 was not made public for twenty-five years, but it remained central to the thinking of the five American presidents of the Vietnam War Era.

guilty verdict, followed by execution or imprisonment.

Ho Chi Minh, as a result of the excesses of the purification campaign, faced a situation in the north that was similar to the one that Ngo Dinh Diem was dealing with in the south—increasing discontent and even some open revolt. One such revolt was put down by force by the North Vietnamese army, the PAVN (the People's Army of Vietnam), under the leadership of General Vo Nguyen Giap. However, to lessen the discontent, in August 1956 Ho publicly apologized to his fellow citizens, saying "errors have been committed,"[32] and released those prisoners whose arrests were

A U.S. officer trains South Vietnamese soldiers. Between 1961 and 1963, the number of U.S. troops in Vietnam increased dramatically.

questionable. He gradually regained the trust of the peasants. However, Ho's errors had given an air of legitimacy to the American position that communism was a horrible system to live under. Ngo pointed with alarm to what communism would mean for Southeast Asia, and the United States used the failed purification program as proof of the nobility and urgency of its efforts to protect the south from communism.

Military Expansion in the South

In 1961, Ngo asked for sufficient U.S. aid to increase his troops from 170,000 to 270,000 to fight the NLF and its combat arm, the Vietnamese People's Liberation

Army (VPLA). Acting on advice of key military advisers, in February 1962, President Kennedy created the Military Assistance Command, Vietnam (MACV), and appointed General Paul Harkins to lead it. From this point forward, the number of Americans serving in Vietnam steadily increased. At the time of Kennedy's assassination in November 1963, the number of American soldiers in Vietnam had grown to 16,300. According to Larry H. Addington, except for some covert operatives, "all MACV troops were [still] officially advisers and technicians, not combat soldiers, though

Combat Villages

The government of the Republic of Vietnam was not the only one to build villages designed to help in the war effort. NLF forces built temporary secret camps where they regrouped, trained, and planned missions. Ordinary villages sympathetic to the NLF also organized themselves into "combat villages," fortified in different ways to protect the NLF and the villagers from discovery and attack. These defenses (particularly early in the war, before the NLF had access to large stores of weapons from Communist allies) were generally crude but very effective. One common device was the "naily board," loosely covered pits filled with sharpened bamboo and metal spikes. Unwary soldiers fell into these pits and were killed by the deadly spikes. One gun used to defend settlements was called a "sky horse." It shot pellets and glass shards dipped in snake venom, which had the same effect on its victims as a deadly snakebite.

The communities also dug extensive networks of tunnels so they could hide or escape quickly. Unlike strategic hamlets, with their fences and watchtowers, "We build our fire positions as close to the ground as possible and the rest underground, because our people are defending their own homes," one guerrilla explains in Marilyn B. Young's *The Vietnam Wars*. During the day, NLF members hid in the fields and jungles, and at night they came into the village to eat, discuss the war, and sleep, if it was safe to do so. Through such methods, life could appear completely normal in these villages yet residents were prepared for immediate action. Many returning American soldiers said one of the most frightening and frustrating things about the war was that there was no way to tell a combat village from any other, to know whether its residents were friendly or ready on a moment's notice to ambush and kill them.

the distinction became ever harder for the Kennedy administration to maintain."[33]

American support was not limited to direct aid to Ngo's Army of the Republic of Vietnam (ARVN) and the presence of advisers and staff. In 1963, Kennedy sent hundreds of helicopters and other equipment to the south, and increased the number of covert operatives there. The Green Berets were the first of these groups, a special force of army soldiers trained to carry out surveillance missions and covert operations to kill VPLA leaders and destroy their hideouts and supply networks. Until this point, to keep the U.S. presence advisory, Americans had been limited to roles on ARVN bases and other locations outside of any potential combat zones. Now, however, Kennedy allowed military advisers to accompany ARVN units in the field. He also allowed U.S. Air Force pilots not only to train Vietnamese pilots but also to fly the planes themselves in support of ARVN ground troops.

Strategic Hamlets

Though during the Kennedy years there were still no combat units sent to Vietnam, U.S. involvement was clearly becoming more substantial. It also remained misdirected due to the manipulative leadership of Ngo. One particular venture, the creation of "strategic hamlets," typifies American cooperation with Ngo during the Kennedy years. Overseen by William Colby, later to become director of the CIA, and directed by Ngo's brother Ngo Dinh Nhu, the idea behind the establishment of strategic hamlets was to protect rural South Vietnamese from the influence of the NLF. The Americans were led to believe that the NLF and its army, the VPLA, were terrorizing villages and forcing people to support it, although there was little evidence that this was true. The idea was to create safe villages where people could live without fear of pressure from NLF "outsiders."

The first step in creating a strategic hamlet was to clear land and enclose it with barbed wire and observation posts. A few concrete administration buildings were then erected. At this point villagers from an area usually many miles distant were rounded up, often at gunpoint, by ARVN soldiers, then forced to march to their new location. American funds paid for the entire operation, including the materials delivered to the site that the villagers were to use to build their new homes. First, however, they were denied access to these materials until they vowed not to run away. At that point, corrupt local army officials would make the villagers buy the materials for their homes, although these materials had been donated by the United States to be provided free of charge to those relocated. "Promised supplies and social services never reached the peasants" either, according to Marilyn B. Young, "however lavishly the Americans supplied them to provincial officials."[34]

By the summer of 1963, official ROV figures indicated that two-thirds of the population was "safe" inside strategic hamlets, under ARVN guard. In fact, only around 10 percent of these hamlets provided any real semblance of security. At night the guards left, leaving the supporters and members of the NLF free to enter the villages, hold meetings, share information, and resupply their units. Furthermore, because they were, in the words of historian Marilyn B. Young, "living in hovels, farming under the impossible restrictions of curfews, subject to searches, arrests and extortion," villagers often "simply left the 'security' of these hamlets to farm their old lands, look after their fruit trees (if they had not been bulldozed) and meet with . . . friends and relatives, even at considerable risk to their lives."[35] Projects such as the strategic hamlets served only to disrupt traditional life, lower the standard of living of the typical peasant, and foster deepening resentment of the United States. Few peasants cared at all for anything beyond their rice paddies and their water buffalo, the tools by which they and their families survived year after year, generation after generation. To them the Cold War was meaningless. They supported the side that promised to make their misery stop and did what they could to undermine the side that caused it.

Ngo Dinh Ngu's security forces brutalized the people of South Vietnam.

A Growing Antipathy

Ngo Dinh Diem and his American supporters were the cause of much of that misery. "Had Ngo Dinh Diem proved a man of breadth and vision," one leader of the opposition said later, "[people] would have rallied to him."[36] As it was, over the years of his regime opposition became only broader and deeper. A major source of people's resentment was Ngo's brother, Ngo Dinh Nhu, who oversaw what ironically were called the ROV security forces, but which in fact, due to their widespread and random brutality, created little security at all for the Vietnamese.

Because these two men were so hated, by the end of 1961 it was no longer possible for government officials or troops to venture anywhere in Vietnam more than a mile or two out of heavily patrolled cities and bases without risk of ambush or sniper fire. This was presented to the U.S. leadership as a sign of the growing strength of communism, which Ngo claimed could be countered only by more and more American aid. Already much of this aid was not going any further than the pockets of the Ngo regime, and even those funds that were being used by the army were not being well spent.

In fact, the overriding reason for growing discontent in the south was Ngo himself. The Kennedy administration had no real enthusiasm for Ngo as a person or a leader, but it saw no other choice but to support him. Historian Frederik Logevall explains that "from the moment of Ngo Dinh Diem's appointment as prime minister in 1954, American officials had been concerned about his shortcomings as a leader. . . . Nevertheless they had stuck with him, partly because they thought his staunch anticommunism . . . might make up for [his] weaknesses, and partly because no adequate replacement appeared anywhere in sight."[37] Logevall goes on to point out that "Sink or Swim with Ngo Dinh Diem" became a popular slogan around the White House.

However, the point at which the United States could no longer look the other way was reached over the regime's unequal treatment of Buddhists and Catholics. Vietnam was approximately 20 percent Catholic, a legacy of the missionaries of the French colonial era. Vietnam was, and had been for centuries, a strongly Buddhist culture. Ngo, however, was from one of the elite Catholic families of the country. His Catholicism, in fact, was one of the reasons U.S. political leaders had thought he might be easy to work with, because Christianity gave them something in common. However, Ngo's Catholicism created a problem in his own country. Ngo favored Catholics heavily over Buddhists. He disproportionately appointed Catholics to government posts and exempted them from participation in building roads and other public projects that was mandatory for others.

The shift in status between Catholics and Buddhists was aggravated by a massive influx of Catholics from the north, who had come south at the urging (and at the expense) of the church as part of a plan to strengthen Ngo's political base. As newcomer Catholics were welcomed by the regime, Buddhists felt even more shoved aside. Provisions allowing the Catholics to own their churches but not allowing the Buddhists to own the temples where they gathered to pray and meditate added to the tension in the country. The extent of Ngo's blindness to or simple lack of concern for his impact on non-Catholics became shockingly clear when he announced the dedication of the ARVN to the Virgin Mary, one of the key icons of Christianity. In the end, it was Ngo's attitude toward the Buddhists that would result in his fall.

The End of Ngo Dinh Diem

In early June 1963, Ngo decreed that traditional flags honoring the Buddha's birthday could not be flown. In response, an old Buddhist monk sat in the traditional lotus position on a busy Saigon street. After permitting an assistant to douse him with gaso-

Thich Quong Duc, a Buddhist monk, sets himself on fire to protest Ngo Dinh Diem's government. When Ngo responded by arresting nearly fifteen hundred monks, the United States removed him from power.

line, the monk, named Thich Quang Duc, lit a match and burst into flames. The incident was filmed by the Associated Press, and the photo of the still-upright monk surrounded in flame with his face blackening and blistering was front-page news around the world. In the next few months, six more monks committed suicide the same way, in protest of the Ngo regime. Diem responded by imposing martial law and invading the two dozen temples where the activist monks were living. Approximately fifteen hundred monks were arrested, a dozen were killed, and many more were injured. Mass public protests broke out as a result.

This turn of events did not play well in the United States. Though many Americans strongly supported the fight against Communist expansion, questions began to be raised in Congress, as well as in American living rooms and church pulpits, about why the United States was supporting a regime that openly and flagrantly violated cherished principles such as freedom of speech and religion. Behind the scenes in Washington, Kennedy and his advisers were coming to the conclusion that Ngo was incapable of controlling South Vietnam and had to be replaced. A means of doing this presented itself when Henry Cabot Lodge, the ambassador to

John Paul Vann

American leaders were frequently lied to about how the campaign in Vietnam was going. Ngo lied about how effective his army was, and these lies were passed along as fact by officers in the field, who often made their own embellishments so as to make it look as if the Vietcong were being outflanked, outgunned, and outfought at every turn.

Not everyone lied, however. One notable exception was Lieutenant Colonel John Paul Vann. Vann had been present at the Battle of Ap Bac, south of Saigon, in January 1963. At that time the United States had only advisers in place, and Vann was working alongside an incompetent Vietnamese colonel, Bui Dinh Dam. Vann advised Bui to send in troops to attack several villages harboring Vietcong guerrillas, but Bui decided to wait a day, giving the guerrillas a chance to learn of the planned attack.

When the soldiers arrived they were ambushed. Vann, watching from a plane, radioed to Bui's superior, General Cao, to send in tanks to rescue the trapped soldiers. He replied that he did not take orders from Americans. The Vietcong disappeared back into the jungle, and Vann urged Cao to send troops after them. Cao would not, saying that he thought the army had fought enough for one day. These experiences and others confirmed Vann's belief that the South Vietnamese military leaders were not capable of winning the war because they did not really want to fight. Indeed it was true that officers were likely to lose their jobs if many of their soldiers were killed, and thus they did not want to risk battle.

Vann made his views public through the news media and tried to alert the president and his cabinet, but he was prevented from doing so by high-ranking officers in Washington. To protest what he felt were cover-ups of the real situation in Vietnam, he resigned his army commission. Vann was no pacifist, but simply wanted the United States to win the war and did not think it could under the circumstances. He continued speaking his mind until his death in 1972. His role in the Vietnam War is documented in the acclaimed book by Neil Sheehan, *A Bright and Shining Lie.*

Vietnam, was approached by several senior officers of the ARVN, who told him confidentially that a few top-ranking officers in Ngo's army were plotting a coup but would go forward only if the United States guaranteed in advance that it would support the officers. Lodge made that guarantee but kept this information secret from Ngo.

The plotters indeed seized control of the government. However, after the coup, Ngo and his brother were herded into the back of a van, where they were both shot. President Kennedy was deeply upset by the deaths. Kennedy had made it clear to the plotters, through Lodge, that the American government would look favorably on a coup to remove Ngo from power, but had not expressly approved his murder. Thus the U.S. government (and himself, Kennedy felt) was not innocent in the murders that had followed, even if it had not sanctioned them. Furthermore, Kennedy felt obligated to back the new government, which was composed of Ngo's murderers. Authors Jeremy Isaacs and Taylor Downing report that Kennedy was "profoundly troubled by the religious and moral implications of what was being done in Vietnam in his government's name."[38]

A few weeks later, on November 22, 1963, Kennedy himself was assassinated. There has been much speculation about what Kennedy would have done in Vietnam if he had lived. Authors Isaacs and Downing point out that "Kennedy had made clear to no one his long term policy for Vietnam." He was, instead, "still reacting to events"[39] rather than formulating policy and seemed to those close to him to be unsure as to how to achieve the objective of stopping communism without more deeply involving the U.S. military.

Kennedy's secretary of defense, Robert McNamara, later wrote in his autobiography that the president privately stated to him that since the South Vietnamese had shown so little ability to defend themselves, it was not a good idea to shed American blood defending them. According to Frederik Logevall, "Kennedy was unhappy with the war, but also committed to it."[40] The question of what Kennedy would have done is only an intellectual one, of course, because he did not live out his term. After November 1963, not only South Vietnam but also the United States would have new leaders, with their own ideas about the defense of South Vietnam.

Chapter 4

An American War

The fall of Ngo Dinh Diem and the quick succession of leaders after him did not have an immediate significant effect on the nature of the conflict in Vietnam. It was still a civil war between different factions within Vietnam. Nevertheless, the United States was deeply involved in keeping an unpopular and illegitimate government in power in the south. From the death of Ngo Dinh Diem onward, historian Frederik Logevall argues, "Vietnam . . . became a top priority, day-to-day foreign policy issue for the United States."[41]

By the time Kennedy was assassinated and Lyndon B. Johnson became president, it was clear that the war against communism in Vietnam could not be won decisively as long as it consisted of nearly constant skirmishes between small units of soldiers on both sides. Nor could it be fought effectively when VPLA forces were so skilled at moving around the country without detection, blending in among noncombatants, hiding in remote areas, and holing up in supportive villages.

Logevall explains that by early 1964, "maintaining the status quo, in which the United States persisted in an advisory role, [and] even tinkering with the existing arrangement by adding a few hundred additional American advisors would not make an appreciable difference."[42] It was decided therefore by the new Johnson administration that a major escalation of American military involvement would be required to turn the tide of the war.

However, there were several important reasons President Johnson hesitated to escalate the war. Already there was a small but growing protest movement on college and university campuses, and a number of political leaders were beginning to question even the current limited level of involvement. Second, Johnson was far more interested in implementing what he labeled the "Great Society," a package of domestic civil rights and antipoverty programs. Johnson knew that the expense of war would leave inadequate funding for these efforts.

The coup leaders who engineered the fall of Ngo Dinh Diem were quickly replaced by two other politicians and military leaders, Nguyen Van Thieu and Nguyen Cao Ky. They saw that America's support, which translated into money in their pockets and power in their country, would continue as long as they professed strong anti-Communist views and could persuade the United States that the key to containment of communism was to spend more and more money strengthening the government of South Vietnam.

The Gulf of Tonkin Resolution

Johnson believed the picture painted by the new leaders of South Vietnam—that guerrilla attacks and other violence in the south were part of Ho's master plan to disrupt and destablize South Vietnam rather than expressions of legitimate discontent. Johnson and his advisers, therefore, drew up plans for an all-out war involving a merciless bombing campaign in the north and the use of American ground troops to go after the VPLA in the south. However, Johnson knew the American people would not tolerate such an escalation without strong provocation. Throughout the first

Nguyen Van Thieu (foreground) and Nguyen Cao Ky (saluting, right) professed strong anti-Communist views in an effort to garner American support.

The Gulf of Tonkin Incidents

On August 2, 1964, the destroyer *Maddox* had been patrolling near the shoreline of North Vietnam doing electronic surveillance, as it had been doing for approximately a month, despite protests by the North Vietnamese that it was in their territorial waters. As it traveled back into international waters, three North Vietnamese torpedo patrol (PT) boats followed it, launching torpedoes and opening fire from their decks. The *Maddox* suffered no significant damage. Tensions were very high onboard, however, as the crew was ordered to continue its spying mission and thus were anticipating more attacks.

When bad weather struck the Gulf of Tonkin two days later, false echoes from the stormy waters led sonar operators to conclude that PT boats were approaching. For several hours, the *Maddox* fired at the spots from which the echoes seemed to be coming, but the storm made it impossible to confirm the PT boats' presence visually. The "battle" was duly reported to Washington, but by the next day the officers in charge had concluded that there had not actually been PT boats in the area. This also was duly reported. Johnson, however, told the American public there had indeed been a second attack. Years later, records of Johnson's briefings on these two Gulf of Tonkin incidents revealed that Johnson himself did not believe the second incident had ever occurred and that he was aware that the first was not an entirely unprovoked attack. Nevertheless, he presented the more convenient versions of what had occurred to get the authority to go to war.

President Johnson announces the second attack on the Maddox *in the Gulf of Tonkin.*

eighteen months of his presidency, Johnson waited for something to happen that would give clearer justification for a more direct combat role for America in Vietnam and in neighboring Laos, whose Communist insurgent group, the Pathet Lao, was serving as a major source of supplies for the VPLA.

That opportunity arose in July 1964. In international waters in the Gulf of Tonkin an American military ship, the *Maddox*, was fired upon by several North Vietnamese patrol torpedo (PT) boats. The circumstances surrounding this encounter, and a reported second attack two days later, were murky and contradictory, but Johnson saw that his moment had arrived. He went on television and stated that "repeated acts of violence against the armed forces of the United States must be met not only with an alert defense but with a positive reply."[43] He then went to Congress and asked it to pass a resolution giving him authority to take whatever steps he as president felt were necessary to fight Communist forces in Laos and in all of Vietnam, painting them as the enemies of peace and freedom in the region. The Gulf of Tonkin Resolution passed unanimously in the House and by a vote of ninety-eight to two in the Senate. It was the closest the United States ever came to an official declaration of war in Vietnam. Johnson now had the ability to use the full resources of the American military in Vietnam.

"Win the War"

This was the first major escalation of what was always officially called a "military action" rather than a war. The escalation came about, ironically, as an effort to end the war. It was hoped that a decisive victory might be quickly achieved by use of overwhelming force, despite the fact that the French had tried the same tactic without success at Dien Bien Phu. Also, at the time of the Gulf of Tonkin incidents, Johnson was at the end of an election campaign in which he had been attacked by his opponent, Barry Goldwater, for being too passive in Vietnam. Johnson, wanting to look capable of making tough decisions, said repeatedly that he was "not going to lose Vietnam" and gave the simplest and most sweeping orders to his generals: "Win the war."[44]

Behind the politics, however, was what had become a constant in American thinking—Cold War fears of the creeping Communist menace. Though military reports were generally favorable, sometimes more than was really accurate, it was still clear that the mightiest nation in the world was not winning the battle for the hearts and minds of the Vietnamese people. That the people of Vietnam would not freely choose the American way of life and governance over the Communist way was incomprehensible to most Americans, as was the ongoing and increasing popular support for the Communist-backed NLF and VPLA.

Asking hard questions about why the Vietnamese thought as they did was not part of Cold War thinking. Put simply, if further incursions of communism in Southeast Asia were to be stopped, the war would have to be won with or without the support of the Vietnamese people. American efforts would be appreciated later, many felt, when Communist brainwashing of the Vietnamese people stopped. The view that Americans were really assisting the Vietnamese to build a better and freer society was important for the Johnson administration to maintain because the planned war was going to make life in Vietnam much worse in the short run. Americans were going to need to believe the cause was just and the duration would be short. In 1965, it still seemed possible to make good on those expectations.

The Bombing Campaign

General William Westmoreland, who was responsible for American combat operations in Vietnam, proposed a two-pronged approach for a quick victory in Vietnam. One prong was an extensive aerial war in the north, and the other was the use of ground troops in the south. The first stage of the bombing campaign was called Operation Barrel Roll. This was designed to destroy the northern stretches of the Ho Chi Minh Trail, by which the Pathet Lao and the PAVN, the armed forces of North Vietnam, assisted each other and sent supplies south to help the VPLA. It was followed by Operation Rolling Thunder, a more extensive bombing campaign against military targets in North Vietnam.

These aerial campaigns lasted throughout the war. They involved far more than bombs. In addition to explosives, the United States dropped tons of napalm, a flammable gel that kills or maims its victims by sticking to clothing and flesh and burning until it reaches bone. American forces also dropped 18 million gallons of herbicides to kill the tropical vegetation in which the VPLA forces hid. It also killed the rice crops all Vietnamese depended on for food. One particularly toxic defoliant was known as Agent Orange, which contained the poison dioxin. It took years for this to be flushed out of Vietnam's soil and rivers, and many believe it caused cancer among Americans and Vietnamese exposed to it. The American bombing campaigns caused many deaths and maimings, destroyed families, and were responsible for wide swaths of dead vegetation, hunger, despair, and increasing anger against the Americans.

The Johnson administration claimed, however, that such tactics were necessary to look tough on communism and thus maintain an edge in the Cold War. The United States could not back down because it would look like lack of resolve to combat world communism, even though, as Jeremy Isaacs and Taylor Downing point out, bombing "was not an effective way to strike at an undeveloped nation where supplies were still transported by bicycle or on the backs of porters."[45] Most Vietnamese still lived in small villages, harder targets to hit than larger population centers, and trails could easily be diverted around bombed-out stretches. Though privately Johnson and his advisers knew that there was no military victory to be achieved by an aerial war, they hoped the devastation might force the north to negotiate a settlement.

An American plane spreads Agent Orange over a North Vietnamese forest in an effort to flush out VPLA soldiers in hiding.

The Arrival of Combat Troops

The strategy to be used against the north had to be limited to aerial bombing and covert operations because using the U.S. Army there would have amounted to an invasion of a foreign country. This would most certainly have provoked a counterattack by the Soviet Union and China, and might possibly have precipitated a global nuclear war. However, in the south, the government of the ROV could be counted upon to welcome as many soldiers as the United States wished to send.

U.S. Marines land on the beach at Da Nang. The marines were part of the first wave of U.S. combat troops to enter Vietnam, a number that increased to 183,000 by the end of 1965.

There, Westmoreland's strategy was to bring in American ground troops to assist the ARVN. He asked for and received from the Johnson administration an increase from approximately 90,000 soldiers, still mostly technicians and advisers, to 175,000, mostly combat troops. The first of these troops, 3,500 marines in full battle gear, came ashore at Da Nang on March 8, 1965. They and the others who followed were there primarily to guard cities and coastal areas while the ARVN fought the guerrilla war in the interior. Without such reinforcements, Westmoreland told Johnson, the ROV would fall within a year.

By the end of 1965, there were 183,000 U.S. combat troops in Vietnam, and Westmoreland had been promised as many more as he felt he needed. Westmoreland's strategy was to search for and destroy enemy bases and means of supply in the south and to splinter the VPLA and PAVN so badly they could not fight effectively. That, it was hoped, would make the north willing to negotiate for a peaceful end to the conflict.

Because the war was likely to consist more of small battles than major campaigns where victory could easily be declared, and because there was to be no invasion of the north or other territorial grabs that would give a clear measure of progress, Westmoreland proposed that success in Vietnam be measured by the body count. If there were many more VPLA and PAVN casualties than American ones at the end of a skirmish, the United States could be said to have won, even if the enemy had successfully melted back into the jungle to fight another day. If the body count of VPLA and PAVN was higher day in and day out, the United States could claim it was winning the war.

This approach to measuring progress was a mistake. In this kind of war, counting the dead did not accurately portray victory or loss because it did not take into account the Vietnamese resolve to liberate their homeland at any cost—dead soldiers did not make them any more likely to surrender. The picture was made even less accurate by inflated body counts on the battlefield. Also, at times all the Vietnamese dead were counted as Vietcong regardless of whether there was evidence indicating they were mere civilians. Thus, even on days when VPLA and PAVN casualties were high, the United States was not really winning the war.

Combat Begins

The first combat in Vietnam involved the Third Marine Amphibious Force. It trapped a regiment of the VPLA, resulting in more than six hundred dead and an equal number of VPLA wounded. Marine casualties were forty-five dead and two hundred injured. This was viewed as a military success by the United States and alarmed the generals of the PAVN forces. They decided to concentrate their efforts on gaining control over an east-west corridor through South Vietnam, to split it in half and possibly cause the collapse of the ROV. General Westmoreland suspected this plan and developed a counterstrategy for dealing with combat over the rugged and mountainous terrain. It relied on helicopters provided by the First Cavalry Division Airmobile, known informally as the First Air Cav. The helicopters were used to transport men and equipment as well as to fire on the enemy with machine guns and rocket launchers. The use of helicopters gave the Americans the ability to strike quickly and move flexibly. Indeed, helicopter use became one of the most characteristic combat strategies of the war.

The First Air Cav saw combat for the first time in the Ia Drang Valley in November 1965. It was the first major battle of the war, lasting over four days. The well-armed and well-prepared PAVN soldiers fought very effectively, killing two hundred Americans and wounding one thousand. Several units had to send "broken arrow" signals back to their base, indicating they were being overrun. They were rescued only when massive air assaults drove off the approaching enemy. However, in the end Ia Drang was viewed as an American victory because the PAVN casualty count was twice as high and they had been forced to retreat across the border into Cambodia.

The ferocity of the fighting was sobering for President Johnson. The most technologically advanced army in the world, using that technology to the fullest, had had difficulty even holding its own in the first battle of the war. General Westmoreland's suggestion was to send many more troops,

Marines count Vietcong casualties. The conflict in Vietnam quickly became a war of attrition.

and Johnson, though concerned about the prospects of a long and bloody conflict, had no other choice, he felt, but to go in even deeper. Over the next two years, the number of soldiers in Vietnam rose to 485,000, and the annual cost of the war had risen to 20 billion dollars. Ia Drang was fairly typical of the kinds of battles that were fought, and horrific combat involving huge arsenals and heavy casualties began to characterize the whole American undertaking in Vietnam.

Struggling to Stay Even

In those two years, between late 1965 and the beginning of 1968, it became increasingly clear that the war in Vietnam could not be won decisively by the United States, although military leaders and the Johnson administration did their best to keep up appearances. The conflict began to be understood as a war of attrition, in which each side tries to win by simply wearing out the resolve of the other side over time. A war of attrition naturally favors those who are on familiar ground. The guerrillas, therefore, were easily able to hide and travel, getting support from local villagers. Most important of all, the Vietnamese were fighting for a cause they felt strongly about—getting rid of Americans and the U.S.-backed regime in the south.

American soldiers had no such investment. Most had been drafted and thus were not serving in Vietnam by choice. As time passed, it was more difficult to see the connection between any legitimate political goal and the devastation of

The Pathet Lao

The Cold War in Southeast Asia was not limited to Vietnam. In fact, the struggle between supporters of communism and the opposing forces of the United States were just as intense in Laos. After World War II, in Laos a Communist-inspired group similar to the Vietminh, known as the Pathet Lao, worked in the same way to create a broad coalition of Laotians fighting against the reestablishment of French colonialism after the Japanese retreat.

Unlike in Vietnam under Ngo Dinh Diem, the Laotians did have a functioning democratic process. The Pathet Lao (meaning Lao Country or Lao Nation) won enough votes to participate in a number of coalition governments in the 1950s. However, as part of the U.S. policy of fighting communism wherever it seemed to be gaining ground, whenever the Pathet Lao did well enough in an election to earn a leadership role in the new government, the CIA worked behind the scenes to support a coup or to otherwise dissolve the government and force a new election. The CIA also stuffed ballot boxes and spread malicious propaganda to try to get anti-Communist candidates elected. Between 1957 and 1965, the CIA was behind the fall of more than one government a year, resulting in much instability in the country. By 1964 the Pathet Lao was completely excluded from the government, and a puppet regime similar to Ngo Dinh Diem's was established.

By then the Pathet Lao was receiving aid from the North Vietnamese to help it gain control of Laos. When the Pathet Lao began wresting more and more land from government control, the U.S. military became secretly involved in direct military action. From 1965 to 1973, the United States dropped more than 2 million tons of bombs on Laos, more than the total dropped on all fronts by both sides in World War II. American efforts to prevent a Communist takeover were unsuccessful. By the early 1970s, the Pathet Lao controlled most of the country. In the spring of 1975, as in neighboring Vietnam, Pathet Lao forces were able to topple the government and take control of Laos.

Vietnamese life and culture. As dissent against the war mounted at home, the feeling that they were risking their lives in a pointless war began to take hold among the American troops. Soldiers continued to fight and die in pitched battles, but the goal seemed to be tied to nothing grander than keeping America from losing ground and face. For individual soldiers the goal became to mark off one day at a time and go home alive, and whole.

A Turning Point at Khe Sanh

The siege at Khe Sanh in January 1968 illustrated well the American dilemma in Vietnam. Khe Sanh was an American military base in the mountainous region near the Laos border. Its airstrip was essential for bringing in troops and supplies because the road to the base, built earlier in the war, was under the control of VPLA forces. Khe Sanh became the first stage of what was to be a major PAVN offensive against the American and ROV forces. This campaign was designed to turn the tide of the war in favor of the north and put a quick end to the hostilities. A ferocious barrage of PAVN rockets, grenades, and other explosives began the attack at Khe Sanh. In the middle of a firefight, PAVN rockets hit the ammunition supply for the base, and the explosion wiped out many of the buildings. Americans were driven out of the village of Khe Sanh and were able to avoid being overrun altogether only by the arrival of two new battalions.

The PAVN did not retreat into the jungle this time, and the siege that followed the initial battle lasted more than two months. Covered extensively by the American media, it was unflatteringly and soberingly compared to the siege of Dien Bien Phu, which had been the turning point in the French war in Vietnam. It did appear as if the U.S. situation was becoming as hopeless as the one the French had faced. Though fighting communism remained the core reason for the war in the Johnson administration, it was clear that worries about Communist expansion had taken a back seat to the more fundamental worry of being militarily disgraced. It was around this time that the Vietnam War became less an ideological crusade against communism than an all-out struggle simply to avoid military defeat, which by this point seemed possible.

The Tet Offensive

The siege at Khe Sanh was only one aspect of the Tet Offensive, which was a thoroughly planned and coordinated attack on approximately a hundred targets in South Vietnam by forces of the VPLA and PAVN. With the Tet Offensive, North Vietnam showed that it intended to do more than simply react to American military activity in Vietnam. It took place over the Vietnamese New Year, known as Tet, a time when hostilities normally ceased for a few days. As Larry H. Addington describes, "Within the first forty-eight hours, communist forces attacked thirty-six of forty-four provincial capitals, mortared or rocketed every major airfield, and battled [American] soldiers in five of the country's six autonomous cities, in sixty-four district capitals and in scores of lesser towns."[46]

The worst fighting, in the city of Hue, lasted several weeks and involved more than a dozen American battalions before the American forces regained control of the city. Another group of attackers succeeded in getting inside the U.S. embassy in Saigon. This symbolic assault, plus the fighting at Hue and the magnitude of the Tet Offensive overall, contributed to growing negativity in the United States toward the war.

The North Vietnamese and the NLF had hoped the Tet Offensive would change the direction of the war by inspiring a popular uprising in Vietnam. It did not work that way. Many of their best soldiers and leaders were killed, and their ability to mount future attacks was temporarily set back. However, before the Tet Offensive, American generals had painted a picture of an outmatched enemy barely hanging on in South Vietnam. The Tet Offensive made it clear that the war was not, as the American public had been assured, almost won. The Tet Offensive was, therefore, a stunning victory in terms of public perceptions of the war in Vietnam, particularly in the United States.

Johnson Bows Out

The Tet Offensive claimed approximately five thousand American lives, and twice as many wounded. Though the casualty figures for the other side were reported to be much higher, this was a tremendous loss for the United States. Despite this, and

American soldiers take cover on the first day of the Tet Offensive. The North Vietnamese launched this surprise attack in January 1968 during Tet, the Vietnamese New Year.

amid growing dissent within Johnson's cabinet, General Westmoreland asked for a staggering two hundred thousand additional troops in order to exploit what he considered enemy weakness in the aftermath of Tet. This would cost 10 billion dollars to accomplish, further undermine Johnson's domestic programs, step up the draft of young men, and otherwise antagonize the American people. Johnson delib-

The Communist World and Vietnam

Conflict between the two major Communist powers, the Soviet Union and China, gave rise to competition over which would be seen as the hero of the Vietnamese Communist struggle for independence and reunification. As a result, arms, ammunition, and military hardware such as patrol boats and aircraft poured into North Vietnam from both countries. Throughout the war, the barely disguised mutual animosity of China and the Soviet Union worked to the military benefit of North Vietnam, but created diplomatic challenges as well. One example of this occurred in 1965, when Soviet premier Alexei Kosygin tried to tie continued Soviet aid to a promise by the Hanoi government to clarify its allegiance to Moscow over Beijing. His offer was rebuffed, chilling the Soviet relationship with Ho Chi Minh from that point forward.

The diplomatic difficulties North Vietnam had juggling the support of China and the Soviet Union were tied to the fact that each had very different goals. Each was concerned that the other not emerge from the war as the primary Communist ally of Vietnam, for it was felt that a Communist Vietnam would be a major political force in Southeast Asia overall after the war. The Soviet Union was interested in peaceful coexistence with the West, a policy known as détente, and to that end it tried secretly on several occasions to get North Vietnam to negotiate a peaceful settlement. This would have been a great diplomatic success for the Soviet Union because it would have made it rather than the United States look like the world's peacekeeper, and it would have strengthened its position as an ally of North Vietnam.

China, on the other hand, encouraged North Vietnam to seek an all-out victory over the United States and to reunite Vietnam under a Communist government. This was in part due to the Chinese belief that a full-scale Communist revolution was in Vietnam's best interests, and that helping them achieve that would create greater loyalty to China than to the Soviet Union. Ho Chi Minh was aware of all this, and played both sides off each other. To Ho, the aid of both countries was welcomed, but Vietnam intended to chart its own unique Communist future.

erated about his options and eventually decided against such escalation. However, news of Westmoreland's request leaked to the media. Even though Johnson had decided against the escalation, public outcry was immediate and intense because it had even been considered.

The extent to which the nation blamed Johnson for the war was soon made clear when he came within a few hundred votes of being defeated in New Hampshire by a relatively unknown peace candidate, Eugene McCarthy, in the first primary before the 1968 presidential election. Sitting presidents usually run unopposed by candidates from within their own party, but soon several others were campaigning to take the Democratic nomination away from Johnson. Johnson was stung also by a call within Congress for a probe into his conduct of the war. His closest advisers began to tell him he should turn the war over to the South Vietnamese and their army and try to negotiate a peace that would allow an American withdrawal.

With no workable plan to win the war, and with political pressure mounting, on March 31, 1968, Lyndon Johnson went on television to tell the American people he would not run for reelection. He had lost the support even of many in his own party. Despite his visions for the nation and his presidency, he had been able to do little else in his elected term beyond managing an unpopular war. He said he had decided to use the rest of his term to try to seek peace, and he pledged no further escalation of the war. Hanoi responded positively to this development, and for a short while it looked as if the end of the war might be in sight. That impression would prove to be very wrong indeed.

Chapter 5

Spiraling Downward

President Lyndon B. Johnson decided not to seek a second term in office for two reasons. First, his popularity had waned due to the war in Vietnam, and it was not clear at all that he would win another term. Also he realized the war would prevent him, even in his second term, from fulfilling his personal goals of making progress in civil rights and reducing poverty in America. He was viewed by many as little more than a callous warmonger, despite the fact that his Civil Rights Act in 1964 was one of the major achievements of the era, and his "War on Poverty" showed much promise of enhancing employment, housing, and education for poor Americans. All these accomplishments were overshadowed by massive antiwar rallies featuring chants of "Hey, hey, LBJ! How many kids did you kill today?"

Peace seemed as far away as ever by the time his successor, Richard M. Nixon, won the presidential election in 1968 on a platform that included what he called a "secret plan" that would bring "Peace with Honor"[47] in Vietnam. This plan had three parts. The first was to continue the process of "Vietnamization" of the war, begun under Johnson, whereby the war effort would gradually be completely turned over to the Vietnamese armed forces, eventually ending the use of American troops. The second was to take steps to defuse the Cold War by trying to establish peaceful coexistence with the Soviet Union and China. The third was a highly controversial escalation of the bombing campaign in the war, to show that the United States meant to win decisively. The overall plan, therefore, focused on making the North Vietnamese feel abandoned by the Soviet Union and China as it pursued a new relationship with the United States, while simultaneously facing a major escalation of hostilities. This secret plan had significant, generally positive results for the Cold War overall, but in the more focused Cold War effort in Vietnam, the increase in military activity had disastrous results.

New Strategy, Old Results

Nixon's promise to end American troop involvement in Vietnam was radically inconsistent with the escalation of the war that followed his election. In order to keep American casualties down while Vietnamization and American withdrawal were in the early stages, emphasis shifted away from "search and destroy" missions in the rural areas of Vietnam. These missions consisted of small groups of soldiers going into suspected strongholds of VPLA or PAVN forces to find enemy hiding places, seize or destroy weapons and other supplies, and kill any VPLA or PAVN guerrillas they found. Many Americans lost their lives in ambushes on these missions, and thus it was important to scale down this aspect of the war.

However, search and destroy missions were the best way to keep hostile forces from building up their numbers and their supplies so they could not be completely eliminated. Nixon's plan was to continue such missions but as part of larger operations providing more substantial backup. Because there were 543,000 troops in

U.S. helicopters lift off for a "search and destroy" mission. Many American troops lost their lives during these very dangerous missions.

My Lai

On March 16, 1968, one of the worst atrocities ever committed by American soldiers occurred in a village known as My Lai, near the South China Sea. There, soldiers of the First Platoon, Company C, of the Eleventh Infantry Brigade deliberately killed at least one hundred and possibly as many as five hundred villagers. Men, women, and children were, without any provocation, murdered by such means as shooting, beating to death, and bayoneting. What made this war crime even more appalling was that superior officers learned of the My Lai Massacre shortly afterward but took no action against the soldiers and covered up the incident.

The My Lai Massacre finally came to light in late 1969, after a returning veteran wrote letters to the Department of Defense and members of Congress, detailing a story he had been told by fellow soldiers. The subsequent investigation revealed who had been in charge at the scene and who else knew about it. Several high-ranking members of the staff of division commander General Samuel W. Koster were court-martialed, and Koster was punished administratively and relieved of duty. However, responsibility fell most clearly on the shoulders of First Lieutenant William L. Calley Jr., the commander of the First Platoon. Calley was accused not only of ordering the murders but of committing 102 murders himself, by herding villagers into a drainage ditch and shooting them. He was convicted and given a life sentence of hard labor. Three years later, in November 1974, his sentence was diminished to a dishonorable discharge and time served, and he was released. Larry H. Addington, in *America's War in Vietnam*, states that the My Lai Massacre "tarnished the American cause in Vietnam at home and abroad as no other event of the war had done," and it contributed greatly to the growing revulsion of the American public toward the war.

First Lieutenant William L. Calley Jr. (right) was convicted of murder for leading the My Lai Massacre.

Vietnam by mid-1969, larger-scale operations that involved simultaneous search and destroy parties on the ground, aerial bombing, and paratrooper missions were possible. General Creighton Abrams had taken over as commander of the United States Military Assistance Command, Vietnam, in June 1968, upon the promotion of General Westmoreland to army chief of staff. He considered such complex, coordinated assaults on a massive scale to be an important part of wearing down North Vietnam's will to continue fighting.

One such assault was called Apache Snow. In May 1969, an airborne brigade, a marine regiment, and an ARVN regiment helicoptered to the Au Shun Valley, near the Laos border. They met fierce resistance from the PAVN, especially in the region of Ap Bia mountain. Control of the mountain changed hands several times over the course of a few days. Several more battalions and brigades had to be called in before the PAVN soldiers were driven over the Laos border. Victory was declared because the two thousand PAVN dead were twice the number lost on the allied side, but the body count of American dead hardly reflected Nixon's promise to scale down the war. Ap Bia mountain was nicknamed "Hamburger Hill" by the American soldiers, because of the carnage there.

The War Expands to Cambodia

If Hamburger Hill could hardly be called a scaling down of the war, neither could the invasion of Cambodia in 1970. The first incursions into Cambodia had actually occurred a year earlier, in 1969. At that time President Nixon ordered illegal bombing raids in areas along the Cambodian border with Vietnam in order to disrupt supply routes into South Vietnam. Records of these raids had been falsified to make it appear as if the bombs were dropped in Vietnam, so as to conceal the escalation of the war from the public.

A strongly anti-Communist coup had overthrown Communist-leaning Prince Noradom Sihanouk as ruler of Cambodia in 1970, but it was not stable and was not expected to last long. Nixon, knowing that the temporary anti-Communist government was not likely to object too strenuously, ordered what he called an "incursion" into the border regions of Cambodia. His goal was to wipe out Communist strongholds in the area, which were used to supply the VPLA. This was an important part of Vietnamization because breaking the supply routes was essential if South Vietnam were to be able to defend itself against the VPLA after the United States withdrew.

The invasion was a short and a shallow one, limited to going no more than nineteen miles beyond the border. Within a week, Nixon publicly announced that all troops would be withdrawn from Cambodia by the end of June, making the total time there only two months. However, a great deal of damage had been done to Nixon's image as one who had promised to end the Vietnam War. The American public as a whole was unconvinced that this was part of a well-designed strategy to bring a prompt end to the hostilities.

Hell No, We Won't Go!

The campaign in Cambodia was not a success. Few guerrillas and supplies were actually found, for the guerrillas had simply moved deeper into Cambodia and were not followed. The invasion of Cambodia also turned many more Americans against the war and the Nixon administration. Antiwar groups had already been staging huge rallies, such as the National Moratorium on the War held simultaneously in fifteen cities on October 15, 1969. Many young men, particularly college students, made the focal point of their protests their insistence that they simply would not do military service in Vietnam. Resisting the draft, sometimes symbolized by public burning of draft cards, was a much publicized way of protesting the war. The expression *Hell no, we won't go* was chanted over and over again at demonstrations throughout the country. Though some antiwar rallies ended in violent clashes with police, most were peaceful affairs, involving mostly college students but also a wide variety of other Americans concerned about the war.

However, with the invasion of Cambodia, antiwar protests escalated, growing louder, larger, and more confrontational. The protests grew as a result of the feeling that the domino theory had been deformed to the point that the aggressor was the United States, toppling its dominoes across Southeast Asia. This was not, for many Americans, an acceptable way for their country to behave. Many had been able to tolerate continuing in Vietnam, although often with no real enthusiasm, simply because it was important for America not to lose a war. This was especially true within the context of the Cold War, for being unable to prevail in a small, remote country did not bode well for being able to stand up to threats from Communist superpowers. However, when it appeared as if Vietnam would be only the beginning of a wider war, even many former supporters of the war began to weaken.

Questioning the Cold War

The issue of what kind of country the United States really was served to underpin the many different protest movements in the United States in the 1960s and 1970s. This growing spirit of national self-examination also led many to reconsider the ideological differences behind the Cold War as a whole. Some of the key political and intellectual leaders of both the antiwar and civil rights movements were supportive of Communist and socialist ideas. Particularly attractive was the emphasis on community and working together toward common goals and shared rewards. Also important was the idea of creating a society where no one is able to exploit or abuse anyone else.

These goals were seen by radical thinkers as inconsistent with the value Americans put on making and spending a great deal of money, and the American way, in their eyes, came out poorly in the comparison. In a capitalist system, those who succeed economically are considered to be entitled to their profits, without much concern for how others may have been harmed by their success. This led many radicals, particular-

Students in San Francisco protest the Vietnam War by turning in their draft cards. As the war escalated, the frequency and intensity of such demonstrations increased as well.

ly the young, to the conclusion that financially successful people were, in the word of the day, "pigs." This included politicians, who were not to be trusted; corporate leaders; wealthy society figures; and the police, who were believed to serve only the wealthy and powerful.

For many of those who felt this kind of suspicion and dislike of the American capitalist system, communism—at least in its simplest, most idealized form—was an attractive alternative. They saw the value of a communal lifestyle, in which competition was not as important as cooperation and sharing was better than owning. Many college students in particular, once exposed to the philosophy of communism, embraced it enthusiastically. Some went to live on communes where people lived without leaders and shared the food they grew and the products they made. There was a gentleness and respect for others in this lifestyle that they found lacking elsewhere, especially in the nightly news from Vietnam.

Though many of those with an affinity for Communist principles "dropped out" to live largely apolitical lives in communes, others expressed their views by being openly supportive of North Vietnam. The most famous of these protesters was actress Jane Fonda, called "Hanoi Jane" by detractors because she made a supportive visit to North Vietnam. Fonda and others felt that North Vietnam should be encouraged to reform along Communist lines if it so chose. They felt there was no reason why people could not live well under such a system, and at any rate the United States had no right to intrude on any other nation's decisions about its destiny. These ideas were very controversial and very threatening to many Americans, especially those who had family members and friends who were serving, or who had died or been wounded, in Vietnam.

Divisiveness at Home

Tensions were already high between supporters and protesters of the war, but the situation soon got worse. On May 4, 1970, two thousand campuses nationwide held antiwar demonstrations. On one of these campuses, Kent State University, in Ohio, the National Guard unit sent to keep order fired on a jeering crowd, killing four students. In Jackson, Mississippi, two more students were killed under similar circumstances two days later. The nation was deeply divided. Some saw these two events as among the darkest days in American history. "A nation driven to use the weapons of war upon its youth is a nation on the edge of chaos,"[48] the presidential commission investigating the incident wrote in its report.

But others thought the protesters had gotten what they deserved. Two days later a group of New York construction workers attacked a group of marchers protesting what was dubbed the "Kent State Massacre." Amid these and other encounters, President Nixon did little to defuse the tension. The problem, as he and his administration saw it, was to get youthful protesters (whom he publicly called "bums") back under control and appropriately respectful of authority. Historian Marilyn B. Young reports that in reaction to the New York workers' attack, "the White House proclaimed the hard hat a symbol of high patriotism."[49]

Historians compare the dissent and divisiveness in the United States during the Vietnam War to that during the Civil War one hundred years before. Many Americans, dubbed "the silent majority" by President Nixon, believed that it was important to support the president and the armed forces.

They felt that the president and his advisers had more information and thus knew best, and that they would always act in the best interests of the country. They believed firmly that communism was a highly undesirable system and that the United States needed to protect itself against it.

They viewed the protest movement as unpatriotic and as a betrayal of the soldiers fighting the war. "America—love it or leave it" stickers blossomed on car bumpers all over the United States. These messages were countered by another: "America—change it or lose it." This second slogan implied that the very notion of what America stood for was at stake. Many thought America's actions in Vietnam were contrary to the democratic principles on which the country had been built. America, it seemed, had come to resemble the invading powers and the colonial forces it had always aligned itself against, in the name of freedom.

Many Americans accepted the official government position on the war. They

National Guardsmen storm Kent State University in May 1970. The confrontation at Kent State was one of several violent encounters between supporters and protesters of the war.

Kent State University

The invasion of Cambodia touched off an unparalleled storm of protest around the United States. A third of all colleges and universities went on strike, with faculty and students alike joining in marches and sit-ins. Several hundred State Department officials signed a letter of protest, and a number of Nixon's top appointees publicly expressed criticism. However, this fury was matched by others resentful of the chaos that mass protest had introduced into American society. One such person was the governor of Ohio, James Rhodes, who, using Cold War stereotypes, called protesters Communists and compared their tactics to those of Nazi storm troopers and the Ku Klux Klan.

When students at Kent State University burned the building housing the ROTC (Reserve Officers' Training Corps), Rhodes sent in the National Guard to keep order. This military presence on campus raised the level of protest, as it was seen as a tactic used by dictatorships to suppress dissent, not as an appropriate means of dealing with students. On May 4, 1970, under great pressure from the hostile campus environment, a National Guard squad opened fire on a group of fifteen students, killing four of them and injuring a number of others. Some of the injured and dead had not even been protesters, but had simply been walking across campus.

These killings and those of two more students at Jackson State University in Mississippi under similar circumstances led to even stronger antiwar protest. The "Kent State Massacre," as some called it, was used as evidence of how the United States had lost its moral compass in fighting the war in Vietnam. Kent State was in some respects the turning point of the war on the home front, because for a growing number of Americans it was no longer possible to have any other goal than to end this sad chapter in American history as quickly as possible.

Kent State students William Schroeder, Allison Krause, Jeffrey Miller, and Sandra Lee Scheuer (from left) were killed by National Guardsmen.

Construction workers rally in support of the Vietnam War. Despite widespread antiwar sentiment, many Americans approved of U.S. involvement in Vietnam.

believed that South Vietnam was a legitimately separate country threatened from the outside by its Communist neighbor North Vietnam. They believed that South Vietnam's leaders had been freely and fairly chosen by the people. They believed these leaders had been chosen to lead the fight against communism because that was what the people of South Vietnam wanted. But as the war dragged on, even Americans who embraced that goal began to wonder why the United States was fighting South Vietnam's war for it. By 1968, a growing number of Americans were no longer willing to accept containment of world communism as an answer.

One of the professed goals of the Cold War was to protect the American way of life. Ironically, the Vietnam War had the unanticipated effect of shaking that way of life to its core. The concept of the human right to "life, liberty, and the pursuit of happiness" and the belief in democratic rule and freedom of expression were inconsistent with images of pulverized Vietnamese cities, anguished refugees, and dead soldiers and civilians on both sides. These ideas were also inconsistent with images of Americans being beaten and even killed for expressing their antiwar views. One popular comic strip of the era, *Pogo*, put the national mood in its most succinct form.

Adapting a famous battlefield quotation, "We have met the enemy and it is ours," one of the *Pogo* characters reports, "We have met the enemy and it is us."

Finding a Way out of Both Wars

The country was in a somber mood as the 1970s began. The Vietnam War seemed to be escalating, not winding down, and protest movements were creating deep antagonisms within American society. Furthermore, the Cold War buildup of huge arsenals of increasingly more powerful weapons created a deep sense of insecurity about the future. Though many international diplomatic efforts had been undertaken over the years to limit the growth of nuclear arms, the relationship between the United States and the Soviet Union was perhaps best symbolized by two huge nuclear devices aimed at each other. In the words of authors Jeremy Isaacs and Taylor Downing, "each side devoted huge resources to developing weapons it hoped never to use."[50] Peace was kept by the certainty of mutual assured destruction if these weapons were ever unleashed. Finding a way to end the Cold War seemed imperative to the future of the world.

It was largely to avoid a nuclear showdown that the war in Vietnam had been so drawn out. The United States had made sure not to use tactics that might have provoked a war with either the Soviet Union or the other Communist superpower, China. Instead, it had relied on close-in fighting and conventional weapons. This had produced a very bloody stalemate and the growing realization that the war would be abandoned by whichever side needed peace most desperately. Nixon's goal, therefore, was not to win the war, but to extricate the United States from it in a way that preserved its dignity and stature in the world. The key to that, Nixon thought, was to take assertive steps to enhance the view of Americans as the architects of a global peace.

An Unexpected Opportunity

Nixon saw that political tensions between China and the Soviet Union, over their mutual borders and their styles of communism, might create an opportunity for the United States to warm up its relationship with both Communist superpowers. They were each likely to view a closer and more productive relationship with the United States as giving them leverage in their struggle for supremacy between themselves.

China and the Soviet Union had always had great philosophical differences in their approaches to communism. Where Soviet doctrine favored expansion of communism to other nations, China favored a focus on implementing what it considered to be a purer and more complete form of communism within its own borders. China was in the middle of what was known as the Cultural Revolution, a time of political and social upheaval and great internal violence in the name of "purification." Authors Jeremy Isaacs and Taylor Downing explain that "To the Soviet leaders, China appeared

Two Changed Countries

With the arrival of American ground troops in Vietnam, life in its cities began to change. As millions of Vietnamese were forced to leave their homes and farms because of bombing and defoliation campaigns, displaced and impoverished people began to construct sprawling shantytowns on the edges of cities. With no skills except farming, which they could no longer do, many found new ways to make a living off American soldiers. Bars, clubs, massage parlors, and similar entertainments became a major part of urban Vietnamese life. American cigarettes, American beer, radios, cameras, shaving cream, and other such items sold at the military post exchange ended up on the black market as the Vietnamese themselves developed a taste for American products.

Though there was now more to buy and do, these changes had an increasingly negative effect on Vietnamese society. Family ties eroded quickly in the shantytowns without a traditional lifestyle to support them. Now Vietnamese could earn more in a week than past generations had made in a year, and because money was so desperately needed, people made decisions based on finances rather than on keeping families strong and intact. Many Vietnamese women became prostitutes, for example, and a few, considered far luckier, became consorts or even wives of American servicemen. When Vietnamese women started giving birth to ethnically mixed children, the reaction was very negative, and the children were often shunned. When sons made money in ways their parents did not approve of, family dynamics also suffered.

But the changes were not all one-sided. American servicemen changed too as a result of their time in Vietnam. The most significant impact of Vietnamese life revolved around the drug trade. Southeast Asia is a major producer of opium, and in addition to copious amounts of marijuana, soldiers had easy access to unlimited supplies of cheap opium and its powerful derivative, heroin. Many developed addictions, which they brought home with them when their tour of duty was over. This new population of addicts greatly expanded the American market for such drugs. As powerful street drugs became more available and more diverse, the seeds of today's epidemic of addictive drug use were sown.

to be wild, anarchic, and unpredictable,"[51] and they were fearful China might try to undermine Soviet power in some fashion. To this end, there had been a massive military buildup and frequent hostilities along the lengthy (and disputed) border between the two largest countries in the world.

Nixon decided that it was time to, as he put it, "play the China card."[52] He and his chief foreign adviser, Henry Kissinger, saw that making a friendly gesture to China might be a means of both reducing Soviet influence in the world and ending the war in Vietnam. The goal of ending the war in Vietnam could be achieved, Kissinger felt, only if North Vietnam was pressured to accept settlement terms. The best way to do that was to get China, an essential North Vietnamese ally, to want peace in Vietnam badly enough to exert this pressure. The best way to get China to want peace in Vietnam was to offer the incentive of a friendlier relationship with the United States in the post–Vietnam War era.

This would all have to be done without antagonizing the Soviet Union, however, with whom the new Cold War strategy of détente was already under way. *Détente*, from a French term signifying keeping something at arm's length, was a philosophy of coexistence based on the new belief that neither side in the Cold War had to overrun the other in order to survive. This new and promising approach to managing the Cold War was important to maintain, and friendliness with China would put friendliness with the Soviet Union at risk, if it were not handled very deftly. It was a complex strategy, but if Nixon could succeed at it, the result could be the conclusion of one war in Vietnam and the beginning of the end of the larger Cold War.

Chapter 6

An End to Two Wars

Nixon's efforts to reach out to China and the Soviet Union in the early 1970s were a major turning point in the Cold War. His immediate goal, however, was the narrower one of ending the war in Vietnam. Nixon vowed, "I'm not going to end up like [President Lyndon Johnson], holed up in the White House afraid to show my face on the street. I'm going to end that war. Fast."[53] Yet, because his efforts to do so were highly secret in their early stages, a gloomy and angry mood about the Vietnam War and anxiety about the Cold War arms race continued to grip the nation throughout Nixon's first term in office.

The year 1970 was a particularly tumultuous and confusing one for Americans. President Nixon, on the one hand, began a substantial withdrawal of troops from Vietnam, then on the other, suddenly invaded Cambodia. The killings at Kent State and the revelation of war crimes by Americans, such as a massacre at the Vietnamese village of My Lai, created further unrest about the war. It was an uneasy year for the Vietnamese as well. South Vietnam seemed incapable of fighting the war on its own, despite how well supplied and well trained Vietnamization might leave them. The north was reeling from the death of its national hero, Ho Chi Minh, of heart disease the year before.

At the same time all of these events were occurring, Nixon's national security adviser, Henry Kissinger, began secret peace negotiations in Paris with North Vietnamese diplomat Le Duc Tho. Kissinger also began secret talks with both the Soviet Union and China, to negotiate better economic and diplomatic relationships with each. Thus, he subtly began the process of approaching the enemy to negotiate a better relationship, known by the French term *rapprochement*. Though the Cold War would not officially end until the fall of the Soviet Union in 1991, from the time of the Nixon administration on, fears of mutual assured destruction began to dwindle. The Cold War was becoming neither as cold nor as warlike as it had seemed two decades before.

Vietnamization Falters

By 1971, signs of hope began to appear that American involvement in Vietnam was indeed winding down. The number of soldiers in Vietnam had dropped from its all-time high of more than a half million to around 156,000 by the end of 1971. However, because America's avowed purpose for being in Vietnam in the first place was the Cold War goal of protecting it from communism, it was not possible simply to abandon South Vietnam, since many Americans still believed in and feared

National Security Adviser Henry Kissinger (left) and North Vietnamese diplomat Le Duc Tho (right) discuss Vietnam's future. In 1970 Kissinger and Le Duc Tho began secret peace talks.

Henry Kissinger

Henry Kissinger was one of the most important personalities in the Cold War. Kissinger's key role as an American diplomat was all the more surprising since he was not born in America. Born in Fuerth, Germany, on May 27, 1923, he came to the United States in 1938 as a teenager, and became a U.S. citizen five years later.

His work as a Harvard professor of foreign policy led him into advisory roles for the Departments of State and Defense and later to several appointments in the Nixon administration. The term *shuttle diplomacy* was invented to describe Kissinger's style of flying from one place to another to meet face-to-face with top world leaders to negotiate settlements of conflict. He played a key role in bringing about Nixon's historic visit to China, as well as establishing friendlier relations with the Soviet Union.

He was awarded a Nobel Peace Prize for these efforts and others and received a number of the highest honors the American government can bestow. These include the Presidential Medal of Freedom (1977) and the Medal of Liberty (1986). However, more recently Kissinger has come under attack for his role in the invasion of Cambodia. As the president's chief foreign adviser, he endorsed massive bombing there as part of an overall strategy for bringing the war in Vietnam to a quick end. Thousands of tons of bombs were dropped, without any apparent attempt to avoid civilian casualties or even to choose targets of military significance. Because this is a violation of international law regarding conduct of war, Kissinger has been branded a war criminal by some. His record of making both peace and war makes him one of the most instrumental and controversial shapers of history during the Nixon presidency.

the potential results of the domino theory. Central to Nixon's goal of peace with honor, therefore, was a successful Vietnamization program. This would enable the United States to say that they had left the South Vietnamese in good shape to protect themselves. In this way, the United States could leave without appearing to have succumbed to softness on communism.

To show that Vietnamization was working, Nixon pressured the Vietnamese president, Nguyen Van Thieu, to mount a campaign against the Communist forces using only South Vietnamese soldiers.

Thieu's generals planned an incursion into Laos to sever the Ho Chi Minh Trail at the town of Tchepone. Their goal was to obstruct the supply route for the VPLA. The offensive was named Lam Son 719, after a famous victory against the Chinese many years before. Operation Lam Son 719 went badly from the beginning, however. Before the ARVN had gotten far from its starting point at the former U.S. military base at Khe Sanh, their way was blocked by the PAVN. Despite repeated efforts over the course of a whole month to break through PAVN lines, the ARVN was unable to do so.

A change in strategy was called for, so ARVN leaders decided to send troops in by helicopter to Tchepone and occupy it that way. But the troops dropped in by helicopter were so threatened by the PAVN that they had to be airlifted to safety within a few days. In an effort to save face, Thieu called the mission a success because the ARVN had briefly occupied the town, and he ordered the troops still stalled on the road to turn around and go home because the operation had been victorious. However, a large contingent of approximately thirty-five thousand PAVN soldiers attacked them as they retreated. This attack was so ferocious that of the seventeen thousand who set out, only nine thousand avoided death or capture.

Vietnamization had been shown to be disastrously inadequate. It was increasingly clear that the ongoing withdrawal of American troops was going to leave the south seriously vulnerable. Yet there was no other choice. Nixon had to end U.S. involvement, to fulfill his pledge to the American people and to bolster his chances for reelection the following year. The best that could be hoped for at this point was a diplomatic solution, an agreement that would allow South Vietnam to continue to exist. But that, of course, would depend largely on the North Vietnamese and how badly they might wish to get the conflict resolved. To date, they had seemed prepared to continue the war of attrition indefinitely.

Triangular Diplomacy

While the future of the war in Vietnam seemed as uncertain as ever, Nixon's overall foreign policy was actually opening up a number of opportunities to create a more peaceful world. Some of the most productive work toward this goal was not focused directly on Vietnam at all, but on the larger picture of the Cold War. An early sign of the beginning of a thaw in the Cold War was a series of meetings begun in Helsinki in 1969. Known as the Strategic Arms Limitation Talks, or SALT, their purpose was to stop the escalation of the arms race between the Soviet Union and the United States. The talks dragged on for years and were suspended frequently, but the fact that they did not disintegrate altogether was an indication that both the United States and the Soviet Union wished for a change in the dynamic between them.

Nixon and his chief foreign adviser, Henry Kissinger, took the gamble that if the Soviet Union knew the United States was striving for closer relations with China, the rivalry between the Soviet Union and

China might cause the Soviets to try harder to reach a quick conclusion to the talks. In this way, they could claim they and not China were the leaders in Cold War diplomacy.

In part to accomplish the goal of wrapping up the talks, plans were laid for Nixon to visit China, an event of great symbolic significance. Both countries wanted to make the Soviet Union nervous about the possibility of an alliance that could undermine its power, and the United States wanted China's help in ending the Vietnam War. In the words of historian Qiang Zhai, "Clearly China was in a serious dilemma. On the one hand, it had to continue its support for [North Vietnam] to . . . maintain its image as a staunch supporter of national liberation movements. On the other hand, it wanted to preserve the emerging rapprochement with the United States."[54]

Nixon's much-heralded trip to China occurred in February 1972. Within a few months of his visit to China, Nixon also visited the Soviet Union, the first sitting U.S. president to do so since the Soviet Union's foundation more than half a century before.

President Nixon (second from right) tours China's Great Wall in 1972. Nixon's visit to China hinted at the possibility of an alliance between the two nations.

While there, he and Soviet leader Leonid Brezhnev signed the first SALT Treaty. With this major thaw in the Cold War, Nixon began to work toward solving his most pressing immediate problem—ending the war in Vietnam.

The key to this would be pressure by both Communist superpowers on the North Vietnamese. Nixon therefore made it clear that the future of Soviet and Chinese relationships with the United States hinged on their willingness to help the United States exert this pressure. Because China and the Soviet Union were financing the PAVN, they were in a very strong position to force the North Vietnamese government to the negotiating table simply by threatening to cut off their financial support. Then, Nixon reasoned, the north would not be able to take advantage of the withdrawal of American troops to make advances into South Vietnamese territory.

An Assault from the North

Though neither country actually cut back on their military support for the government

Nixon in China

In October 1970, President Richard Nixon made a surprising public statement for a politician who had made his reputation on his strong anti-Communist stance. In an interview in *Time,* he stated, "If there is anything I want to do before I die, it is to go to China." Less than a year later, his close adviser Henry Kissinger made a secret trip to Beijing, the first ever by an official of the U.S. government since China had become a Communist nation. It was so secret that Kissinger had to be smuggled in and out of China through Pakistan, and even Nixon's first secretary of state, William Rogers, did not know about the trip. Among the subjects discussed in China was how to work together to end the war in Vietnam.

After this meeting President Nixon accepted an invitation to visit China in February 1972. Live television coverage was beamed back to the United States, where audiences saw Mao Tse-tung toast the president in the Great Hall of the People in Tiananmen Square and saw Nixon and his wife stroll atop the Great Wall of China. The visit was meant to be symbolic, and no major decisions were reached regarding Vietnam, but it was nevertheless one of the great diplomatic successes of the century. It made a statement that the two ideologically opposed countries had common interests and might be able to work together. It was one of the finest moments of Nixon's presidency and a real victory for détente.

of the PRVN, the north saw clearly that the new linkages between the United States and the Soviet Union and China would cause problems for them in the future. Their Communist allies had let them down once before at the time of the Geneva Accords, when they had allowed the division of Vietnam in the first place and thus set in motion a long and bloody conflict. They knew that neither the Soviet Union nor China would jeopardize their own chances for a better relationship with the United States simply to gain a Communist victory in a land of as little practical significance as South Vietnam. Realizing that they might soon lose the resources necessary to wage a military offensive, the North Vietnamese military leadership decided that it needed to push quickly and decisively to topple the government of the ROV and win a total victory in the war.

With the number of American troops now down to ninety thousand, most of them in noncombat positions, in March 1972, the PAVN mounted a huge assault on the demilitarized zone between North and South Vietnam. They were successful in putting the ARVN on the run and had conquered South Vietnam nearly all the way to the city of Hue before a counteroffensive was launched by the United States. Nixon had tried to stick with Vietnamization, providing massive supplies and arms to the ARVN as it fought to keep the PAVN from advancing, but the ARVN clearly was outmatched. Nixon felt forced to order a new bombing campaign on the PAVN's supply routes, and the port at Haiphong was bombed and mined to keep Soviet supplies from arriving.

The American bombing campaign, known as Operation Linebacker, continued for five months, during which more than forty thousand bombing missions were flown. It targeted the capital city of Hanoi in order to put greater psychological pressure on the country's leadership to seek peace. In the meantime, Soviet president Nikolai Podgorny visited Hanoi to pressure the government to reach a settlement in the war, and Chinese pressure was equally intense. In August 1972, less than two months after Nixon's visit to Moscow, and only six months after his visit to Beijing, the North Vietnamese government voted to authorize Le Duc Tho to finalize a settlement.

Believing an end to the Vietnam War would ensure victory in the November 1972 election, Nixon hoped to reach this settlement before it was held. However, Nguyen Van Thieu, the president of South Vietnam, who had not been consulted, refused to go along when a tentative settlement was reached because, among other things, he would have to leave power. A peace agreement was impossible without him, but Henry Kissinger was able to say on television "we believe peace is at hand"[55] only a few days before Americans went to the polls.

A Bloody Prelude to Peace

An end at least to the American involvement in Vietnam was indeed at hand, but there was still great violence and bloodshed to come. Shortly after his reelection, Nixon ordered Operation Linebacker II, the most intense bombing campaign ever in the Vietnam War, as a way of keeping

A U.S. plane drops bombs over North Vietnam. President Nixon ordered an intense air bombing campaign in the months before America pulled out of the war.

the pressure high to conclude a peace. The north fought back vigorously as well, with massive antiaircraft weapons supplied by the Soviet Union and China. Twenty-nine American bombers were lost, and more than three dozen pilots and crew members were killed and another three dozen taken prisoner after being shot down in this final campaign. All in all, between 1969 and 1973, the years between Nixon's promise to reach peace in Vietnam and the end of the war, more than fifteen thousand Americans died in Vietnam. In this time period, more than one hundred thousand ARVN soldiers also died and as many as four hundred thousand enemy soldiers.

The Paris Peace Accords

Despite the carnage, Operation Linebacker II was indeed successful at getting negotiations back on track. The Paris Peace Accords were finally signed on January 27, 1973, marking the official end of the war. The accords included recognition that Vietnam was one country, and that the north and south would at some unspecified point in the future, by a collective democratic process, determine Vietnam's political destiny without interference by the United States or any other power.

However, it also formally recognized that despite the historical unity of Vietnam, at that point North Vietnam and South Vietnam were different sovereign nations and that both had to be respected as such. It also recognized that territorial and political divisions within the south made it unclear who should rule South Vietnam. Thieu controlled only the area around Saigon. The newly conquered areas of South Vietnam were controlled by the newly created Provisional Revolutionary Government (PRG), as the South Vietnamese Communists now referred to themselves. The accords called for the various factions to put together a free and open election to choose one government for all South Vietnam.

The accords also decreed that none of the various armed forces within Vietnam—the ARVN, PAVN, and VPLA—could increase their numbers, add to territory under their control, or accept any form of outside assistance while the future of South Vietnam was being decided. Furthermore, the North Vietnamese government agreed not to attempt to reunite Vietnam by force as long as the Saigon government abided by the accords. It is unlikely the U.S. government actually thought all of these terms would be enough to prevent the fall of the Thieu government and the eventual collapse of South Vietnam, but the Paris Peace Accords provided a means for an exit from Vietnam that Nixon could call his promised peace with honor.

Neither the North or South Vietnamese governments had much faith in the accords either. The north, despite forcing the withdrawal of the mightiest nation on Earth, had not achieved its goal of reunifying the country. In the words of historian Marilyn B. Young, "millions of refugees, hundreds of thousands of dead, uncounted wounded, the devastation of the countryside north and south, the [destruction] of rural [life] in the south, the [bombing of industries] in the north, the corruption of the urban south, and the prostitution of tens of thousands of Vietnamese women were a heavy price to pay"[56] for nothing more than a sharing of power in the south. Yet the PRV knew that the terms of the peace would probably be temporary because it was not likely that Thieu would honor them. By being patient, they hoped they would be in a position after the American departure to push for their ultimate goal, a unified Vietnam under Communist rule.

Mistrust prevailed in Vietnam. The north doubted Thieu's intentions to uphold the accords, while Thieu was concerned the United States would not uphold its promises to his regime. President Nixon told Thieu he had his "absolute assurance that if Hanoi fail[ed] to abide by the terms of this agreement" it was Nixon's intention "to take swift and severe retaliatory action."[57] That reassurance was reinforced by a billion dollars in additional arms and supplies to South Vietnam before the accords went into effect. Faced with little choice in the matter, Thieu eventually signed the accords, but never intended to abide by them. In recent months he had reclassified many prisoners of war as common criminals so he would not have to give them back in the mandated prisoner exchange, and he had ordered the indefinite detention of every person his army could find who had links to the NLF. The day after signing the Paris Peace Accords, which included an agreement to avoid further violence, he told his troops, "If Communists come into your village, you should immediately shoot them in the head," and if someone began "talking in a communist tone, [he] should be immediately killed."[58]

Hostilities Resume

By this point, however, the most important thing to President Nixon was not Thieu's state of mind, but getting the last troops home. That was accomplished on March 29, 1973. The final group of American combat troops to leave Vietnam included 591 released prisoners of war. For the Vietnamese, however, the casualties would continue to mount for two more years.

The Paris Peace Accords, like the 1954 Geneva Accords they so closely resembled, were not honored for long. They called for the convening of a National Council of Reconciliation and Concord, made up of the warring factions in the south, to plan and carry out elections and monitor the cease-fire. However, mistrust was so high that the group fell apart. Adding to the difficulty was the fact that the accords had overlooked the importance of agreeing upon who controlled what land in South Vietnam at the time of the signing. After the last American troops left, Thieu immediately denied that the PRG controlled any of South Vietnam. When the international group commissioned to establish the agreed-upon demarcation line went out to survey the area, Thieu sent his air force out to bomb them.

Ignoring the clear distinction between the accords he had signed and his actions, Thieu simply began restating what were called his "Four No's": no demilitarization of South Vietnam, no recognition of North Vietnam, no coalition government, and no surrender of territory. The north tried at first to follow the accords as closely as possible. All anti-Thieu forces in the north and the south were told to follow, for the time being, what they called the "Five Forbids." They were not to attack the enemy in any way, resist land grabs by counterattacking ROV forces, lay siege to ROV outposts, shell these outposts, or build combat villages. Despite the Five Forbids, conflict was constant, and in the next two years approximately 160,000 soldiers died on both sides combined. Tens of thousands of civilians perished, and hundreds of thousands more became refugees.

The North Vietnamese's strategy was to see what support Thieu was really likely to have from the United States. Within

The Pentagon Papers

On June 13, 1971, the first installment in a series that would come to be known as the Pentagon Papers appeared in the *New York Times.* These were excerpts from a classified document authorized by Secretary of Defense Robert McNamara in 1967. The document was officially titled "History of U.S. Decision-making Process on Vietnam, 1945–1967," and its purpose was to provide information to future secretaries of state and key advisers. It was never meant for public viewing. However, one of those involved in preparing the document, Daniel Ellsberg, a former Defense Department official, was so disgusted by what he learned that he leaked a copy to the *New York Times.*

The Pentagon Papers revealed that the Truman, Eisenhower, Kennedy, and Johnson administrations had knowingly exaggerated the political and military situation in Southeast Asia to get the public and the Congress to go along with a war in Vietnam. According to Larry H. Addington in *America's War in Vietnam*, such secrecy and manipulation "had become a dangerous influence on the democratic traditions of the United States, and that not national security but the arrogance of those in power was at the root of the problem." Though Nixon had just been elected and thus was not included in the Pentagon Papers he was so alarmed by what they exposed that he sought an injunction to stop their publication. The newspapers countersued, and the matter was eventually decided by the U.S. Supreme Court. It sided with the newspapers, saying that it is important that the press not be restrained in truthfully reporting matters of such great significance and that in fact it was their job, as envisioned by the founders of the American republic, to do exactly what they had done.

Daniel Ellsberg (left) leaked the Pentagon Papers to the New York Times.

a year it was clear that Thieu had been largely abandoned. This was not really Nixon's wish, however. He had wanted to end the killing of Americans in Vietnam, but he did not want to stop or slow down the fight against communism in Southeast Asia. Still a strong believer in the domino theory, he had continued a ferocious aerial bombardment campaign against Laos and Cambodia to show that, despite the end of the war in Vietnam, the United States was still committed to fighting Communist expansion in Southeast Asia. The American public, however, no longer shared his Cold War attitude. Détente with the Communist superpowers seemed an entirely adequate way of dealing with any legitimate threat to the United States from communism, and the tactic of bombing Laos and Cambodia to contain Communist expansion had little support among any but the most rabidly anti-Communist Americans.

Henry Kissinger (second from left) and Le Duc Tho (foreground) sign the Paris Peace Accords in 1973. Even after the peace agreement had been signed, however, hostilities in Vietnam continued.

As a result of the overriding need of the American public to put the war in Southeast Asia behind them, Congress moved to limit Nixon's ability to wage war any further. A bill was passed forbidding any American funding of aerial missions in Southeast Asia. The last U.S. bomb was dropped in Cambodia in August 1973. Then, in November 1973, Congress passed the War Powers Act, called by Larry H. Addington "the most permanent legal consequence of the war."[59] The War Powers Act forbade any American president from using combat troops anywhere in the world for more than thirty days without justifying their use to Congress. If Congress did not agree, the president had only another thirty days to withdraw them. A third blow to Nixon's ability to wage further war was a congressional ban on any funding of any military activity anywhere in Southeast Asia. Nixon was thus unable to fulfill any promises of support to Thieu.

The Fall of South Vietnam

The NLF and the North Vietnamese had not been idly watching the support for Thieu dry up. All along they had been planning a campaign by which they would finally fulfill their main objective of unifying Vietnam. In 1974 they built roads to facilitate communications and movement of supplies, linking the north with the PRG territories in the south. In December 1974, General Vo Nyugen Giap and his South Vietnamese counterpart leading the PAVN/VPLA combined forces set out on a campaign to conquer the five northernmost provinces of South Vietnam.

Giap had not expected a quick victory, but he had not fully realized the depth of disarray in the south. ARVN troops had been depleted by 40 percent, largely due to desertions, and much of the military aid from the United States had been spent by then, or had gone into the pockets of ROV leaders. Within less than a month, VPLA and PAVN forces had conquered the Central Highlands without any reaction from the United States. By mid-March they had advanced to the South China Sea, occupying Da Nang, one of the key American military bases during the war. Their quick success caused them to revise their strategy and try to conquer the rest of Vietnam before the rainy season, which began in May.

In April, Thieu abruptly resigned and escaped to Taiwan. The United States began an emergency evacuation campaign for the five thousand American embassy staff and their families living in Saigon. Also included in the evacuation were close to forty thousand Vietnamese whose service to Americans or the ROV would make them likely victims of retaliation when the ROV fell. The PAVN/VPLA advance on Saigon was so rapid that, in the last few days of April, the pace of evacuation was inadequate despite a fleet of helicopters hastily sent from a fleet stationed in the China Sea. Many people were left behind, and some died after falling from helicopters to which they clung as they lifted off. On April 30, the U.S. ambassador and the last few marines guarding the heliport on the roof of the embassy boarded a helicopter and lifted off, just ahead of a mob that had

Vietnam Today

When the north and south were unified after the fall of South Vietnam, Hanoi became the country's capital and Saigon was renamed Ho Chi Minh City. But other changes were more difficult to make because the country had little modern history of self-rule and had to learn how to govern itself. The nation remained very poor and isolated from most of the outside world through the mid-1980s. At that point, Vietnam implemented reforms that blended elements of communism with free enterprise, and as a result the economy continued to improve slowly and the standard of living improved.

In 1994 the United States reached a milestone in its recovery from the war by lifting a trade embargo and normalizing trade with its former enemy. Since that point, Vietnam's economy has improved greatly. Among its major industries and products are rice, rubber, textiles, food products, and chemicals. By U.S. standards, most Vietnamese are still very poor, but more citizens than in previous years, from farmers to shopkeepers, have moved beyond mere survival.

Though the name Vietnam still conjures up associations with war rather than vacations, recently Vietnam has emerged as a major tourist destination. Its island-studded bays, jungles, mountains, and ancient archaeological wonders draw larger numbers each year. Among the tourists are Vietnam War veterans for whom returning to Vietnam is an emotionally intense experience. Many are able to experience the beauty of the country and the culture for the first time, and to see the Vietnamese as a friendly, peaceful people.

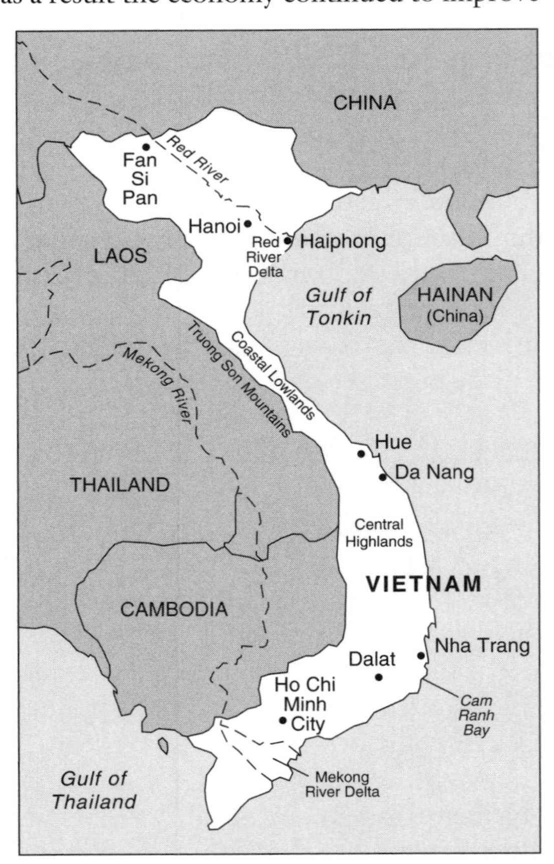

already broken into the embassy below. They were the last Americans to leave Vietnam. Later that day, victory over the ROV was declared and the long war to unify Vietnam finally came to an end.

The End of the Cold War

This did not, however, mark the end of the Cold War. It did not even mark the end of American attempts to stop the expansion of communism around the world. It did signal the end of sustained open military campaigns based on the Cold War logic of fighting communism. In the end, the United States never did find a diplomatic way out of the Cold War, despite a growing realization that the domino theory was not accurate. The Cold War ended as a result of the fall of the Soviet Union in 1991. However, long before this occurred, the battle of ideologies at the heart of the Cold War had taken a backseat to the more pressing need for the United States simply to look politically and militarily strong. Americans had stopped talking about a Communist takeover of the world, and in fact with the success of détente, they even stopped worrying so much about mutual assured destruction. It did not matter so much what the Communist superpowers believed or how people lived there. All that mattered was that the United States could match or exceed their power.

Life in the United States was peaceful after the Vietnam War, but nevertheless, many countries continued to suffer the effects of the continuing Cold War. U.S. involvement in the Cold War from 1975 on was largely covert, focusing on overthrows of unfriendly governments. It was also indirect, taking the form of massive foreign aid to friendly governments. The Cold War thus continued to be a destabilizing force around the world, as many governments as corrupt and self-serving as that in South Vietnam were helped to retain power by whichever side they allied themselves with in the Cold War. The idea of true national self-determination was no more respected by either the Communists or the Americans in Central and South America, Africa, and the Middle East than it had been in Southeast Asia. And so the Cold War continued, until there was no Soviet Union to be allied against.

According to historian Mark Philip Bradley, "The Cold War . . . ended not in April 1975 with the victory of the Vietnamese revolutionaries over the South Vietnamese regime, but in August 1995,"[60] with the establishment of diplomatic relations between the United States and Communist Vietnam. Diplomatic relationships, which include maintaining embassies, are an important means of declaring friendship between two countries, and withholding diplomatic relations is a key way nations express displeasure or antagonism toward each other. Thus, the opening of embassies and similar actions between the United States and Vietnam brought full closure to the conflict.

But over the years, the desire to process what happened in Vietnam and why has been a compelling one. Kennedy's secretary of defense, Robert McNamara, one of the architects of the war, wrote in his 1995 memoirs that the United States was "wrong, terribly wrong,"[61] to have gone to war in Vietnam. However, the factors that caused it on both sides—pinning national survival on military superiority and claiming to be making a better world by forcing one nation's ideology on others—continue to dominate foreign and military policy today. As a result, the world seems to many to be no warmer, and no closer to peace, than it did when the Communists seemed to be painting the map of the world red.

Notes

Introduction: Flawed Vision, Fatal Path

1. Quoted in Loren Baritz, *Backfire*. Baltimore, MD: Johns Hopkins University Press, 1998, p. 42.
2. Quoted in Baritz, *Backfire*, p. 42.
3. Marilyn B. Young, *The Vietnam Wars, 1945–1990*. New York: HarperPerennial, 1990, p. 73.
4. Robert Mann, *A Grand Delusion: America's Descent into Vietnam*. New York: Basic Books, 2001, p. 3.
5. Quoted in Jeremy Isaacs and Taylor Downing, *Cold War: An Illustrated History 1945–1991*. Boston: Little, Brown, 1998, p. 218.

Chapter 1: The Cold War Comes to Southeast Asia

6. Quoted in Larry H. Addington, *America's War in Vietnam*. Bloomington: Indiana University Press, 2000, p. 28.
7. Quoted in Young, *The Vietnam Wars*, p. 11.
8. Quoted in David W. Levy, *The Debate over Vietnam*. Baltimore, MD: Johns Hopkins University Press, 1995, p. 29.
9. Baritz, *Backfire*, p. 60.
10. Baritz, *Backfire*, p. 62.
11. Quoted in Young, *The Vietnam Wars*, p. 15.
12. Quoted in Addington, *America's War in Vietnam*, p. 33.
13. Addington, *America's War in Vietnam*, pp. 37–38.
14. Quoted in Mark Philip Bradley, *Imagining Vietnam and America: The Making of Postcolonial Vietnam, 1919–1950*. Chapel Hill: University of North Carolina Press, 2000, p. 179.
15. Young, *The Vietnam Wars*, pp. 22–23.
16. Addington, *America's War in Vietnam*, p. 38.
17. Addington, *America's War in Vietnam*, p. 34.

Chapter 2: The Grasshopper and the Elephant

18. Baritz, *Backfire*, p. 7.
19. Levy, *The Debate over Vietnam*, p. 30.
20. Young, *The Vietnam Wars*, p. 30.
21. Quoted in Young, *The Vietnam Wars*, p. 33.
22. Young, *The Vietnam Wars*, p. 33.
23. Baritz, *Backfire*, p. 83.
24. Quoted in Addington, *America's War in Vietnam*, p. 41.
25. Addington, *America's War in Vietnam*, p. 42.
26. Young, *The Vietnam Wars*, p. 37.
27. Qiang Zhai, *China and the Vietnam Wars, 1950–1975*. Chapel Hill:

University of North Carolina Press, 2000, p. 64.
28. Young, *The Vietnam Wars,* p. 45.
29. Quoted in Young, *The Vietnam Wars,* p. 52.

Chapter 3: "By All Means Short of War"

30. Quoted in Young, *The Vietnam Wars,* p. 26.
31. Qiang Zhai, *China and the Vietnam Wars,* p. 73.
32. Quoted in Addington, *America's War in Vietnam,* p. 54.
33. Addington, *America's War in Vietnam,* p. 62.
34. Young, *The Vietnam Wars,* p. 85.
35. Young, *The Vietnam Wars,* p. 84
36. Quoted in Young, *The Vietnam Wars,* p. 71.
37. Frederik Logevall, *Choosing War: The Lost Chance for Peace and the Escalation of War in Vietnam.* Berkeley: University of California Press, 1999, p. 5.
38. Isaacs and Downing, *Cold War,* p. 212.
39. Isaacs and Downing, *Cold War,* p. 212.
40. Logevall, *Choosing War,* p. 38.

Chapter 4: An American War

41. Logevall, *Choosing War,* p. xiii.
42. Logevall, *Choosing War,* p. 405.
43. Quoted in Addington, *America's War in Vietnam,* p. 76.
44. Quoted in Isaacs and Downing, *Cold War,* p. 213.
45. Isaacs and Downing, *Cold War,* p. 218.
46. Addington, *America's War in Vietnam,* p. 117.

Chapter 5: Spiraling Downward

47. Quoted in Addington, *America's War in Vietnam,* p. 125.
48. Quoted in Isaacs and Downing, *Cold War,* p. 274.
49. Young, *The Vietnam Wars,* p. 248.
50. Isaacs and Downing, *Cold War,* p. 231.
51. Isaacs and Downing, *Cold War,* p. 272.
52. Quoted in Isaacs and Downing, *Cold War,* p. 273.

Chapter 6: An End to Two Wars

53. Quoted in Mann, *A Grand Delusion,* p. 625.
54. Qiang Zhai, *China and the Vietnam Wars,* p. 203.
55. Quoted in Isaacs and Downing, *Cold War,* p. 281.
56. Young, *The Vietnam Wars,* p. 274.
57. Quoted in Young, *The Vietnam Wars,* p. 277.
58. Quoted in Young, *The Vietnam Wars,* p. 279.
59. Addington, *America's War in Vietnam,* p. 153.
60. Bradley, *Imagining Vietnam and America,* p. 188.
61. Quoted in Logevall, *Choosing War,* p. xiii.

Important Dates

1941
Vietminh founded.

1945
Potsdam Conference temporarily divides Vietnam along seventeenth parallel.
Japanese surrender ends hostilities of World War II.
Ho Chi Minh declares independence of Vietnam.

1946
Vietnam becomes free state within French Union; some French troops return.
Vietminh attack on French in Hanoi begins war of resistance against French.

1948
Bao Dai named head of State of Vietnam.
United States provides first funds to France to fight communism in Vietnam.

1950
Ho Chi Minh government recognized by the Soviet Union.
Bao Dai government recognized by United States.

1954
Battle of Dien Bien Phu.

1955–1956
Ngo Dinh Diem establishes control over Republic of Vietnam. U.S. military advisers arrive in South Vietnam.

1960
Establishment of NLF.

1961
U.S. military personnel increase to more than three thousand.

1962
Strategic hamlet program begun.
U.S. military personnel number over eleven thousand.

1963
Buddhist self-immolation protests.
Ngo Dinh Diem assassinated.
President John F. Kennedy assassinated.

1964
General William Westmoreland becomes head of military operations in Vietnam.
Gulf of Tonkin incident leads to Gulf of Tonkin Resolution.
U.S. military personnel number more than twenty-three thousand.

1965
Operation Rolling Thunder begins; first U.S. combat troops arrive.
U.S. military presence increases to 184,000.

1966
Public hearings on war begin in United States.

U.S. military presence increases to 362,000.

1967

Major peace demonstrations continue across United States.

U.S. troops increase to 485,000.

1968

Siege of Khe Sanh.

Tet Offensive changes public perception of the war.

Johnson decides not to run for president.

Nixon elected president.

U.S. troops number 535,100.

1969

Secret bombing of Cambodia begins.

Nixon announces first withdrawal of twenty-five thousand American troops.

Ho Chi Minh dies.

Massacre at My Lai exposed.

1970

Kissinger and Le Duc Tho begin secret peace talks in Paris.

Congress bans U.S. troop involvement in Laos and Cambodia.

U.S. troops decline to 334,600.

1971

U.S. military presence down to 156,000.

1972

Nixon visits China.

Peace talks break down and resume again.

U.S. military presence down to 24,200.

1973

Peace agreement signed.

Prisoners of war exchanged.

Last U.S. soldiers leave Vietnam.

Congress bans further use of funds for military action anywhere in Southeast Asia.

1975

South Vietnam falls to PAVN forces.

1978

President Jimmy Carter announces normalization of relations with China.

1991

Dissolution of the Soviet Union marks end of Cold War.

1995

Full diplomatic relations restored between Vietnam and the United States.

Glossary

ARVN: Army of the Republic of Vietnam. The South Vietnamese national army.

colonialism: A policy by which a nation maintains or extends its military and political control over a foreign country.

Comintern: An association of Communist parties of the world.

détente: The policy of increasing diplomatic, commercial, and cultural contact with a rival power as a result of a desire to reduce tensions.

domino theory: The belief that if one country became Communist, its neighbors would follow, like a toppling row of dominoes.

draft: The means by which a person is selected for compulsory military service.

free world: Term used to identify non-Communist nations during the Cold War.

guerrilla: A member of an irregular military or paramilitary unit operating in small groups in occupied territory to harass and undermine the occupying force by such means as surprise raids.

howitzer: A kind of cannon.

mortar: A kind of cannon.

nationalism: Devotion to the interests or culture of one's nation. Desire for national independence in a country under foreign rule.

NLF: National Liberation Front. The term for the overall resistance effort within South Vietnam against its government.

PAVN: People's Army of Vietnam. The North Vietnamese national army.

purification: Term used by Communist governments to describe the process by which people and activities deemed anti-Communist are purged from society.

regime: A political administration or system, usually used for governments considered oppressive.

ROV: Republic of Vietnam. Official name for South Vietnam after the removal of Emperor Bao Dai.

siege: The surrounding and blockading of a city, town, or military site by a force attempting to capture it.

SOV: State of Vietnam. Official name for South Vietnam under the leadership of Bao Dai.

Vietcong: Name for the Communist soldiers of Vietnam, used extensively by the United States.

Vietminh: The original name for the

organized effort to rid Vietnam of colonial powers.

Vietnamization: Term coined to describe the process by which the defense of South Vietnam would be turned over to the Vietnamese.

VMLA: Vietminh Liberation Army. The original name for the military wing of the Vietminh.

VPLA: Vietnamese People's Liberation Army. The military branch of the NLF.

For Further Reading

Books

Dale Anderson and Northam Anderson, *The Cold War.* Milwaukee, WI: Raintree, 2001. Thorough but clear discussion of all aspects of the Cold War, including Vietnam.

Kathlyn Gay, *Vietnam War.* Brookfield, CT: Millbrook Press, 1997. Concise and evenhanded discussion of the Vietnam War.

Victoria Sherrow, *Joseph McCarthy and the Cold War.* San Diego: Gale Group, 1998. A biography of one of the key figures in the development of the U.S. Cold War attitude toward communism.

Charles Wills, *The Tet Offensive.* Englewood Cliffs, NJ: Silver Burdett, 1989. Discussion of the events and significance of the Tet Offensive.

Websites

CNN Interactive (www.cnn.com). A comprehensive website produced in connection with the acclaimed series *The Cold War.*

National Archive Learning Curve (http://learningcurve.pro.gov.uk). Developed to complement Great Britain's school curriculum, this website is organized around key questions and provides film footage, documents, and discussion to help students answer these questions.

Studying the Vietnam War Online (www.refstar.com). Excellent website using a study-guide format with links to articles, interviews, and other sources that help students understand the war.

Vietnam Online (www.pbs.org). Developed to accompany *Vietnam: A Television History,* the award-winning PBS series, this website contains documents, discussion, photos, and transcripts of programs.

The Vietnam War (www.vietnampix.com). Contains many award-winning photos by Tim Page, along with discussion of the war in Vietnam and at home.

Vietnam War Index (www.spartacus.schoolnet.co.uk). Contains short, encyclopedia-style articles on key figures, events, and other aspects of the war.

The Vietnam War Internet Project (www.vwip.org). Provides a wide range of information and links. Includes memoirs of participants.

Works Consulted

Books

Larry H. Addington, *America's War in Vietnam*. Bloomington: Indiana University Press, 2000. Concise history of the war in Vietnam.

Loren Baritz, *Backfire*. Baltimore, MD: Johns Hopkins University Press, 1998. Well-written book about how American culture and assumptions led the country into war.

Mark Philip Bradley, *Imagining Vietnam and America: The Making of Postcolonial Vietnam, 1919–1950*. Chapel Hill: University of North Carolina Press, 2000. Excellent discussion of Vietnam's views of and relationship with the United States from 1919 to 1950.

H. Bruce Franklin, *Vietnam and Other American Fantasies*. Amherst: University of Massachusetts Press, 2000. A brilliant, if quirky, retelling of American perceptions of the war, showing how American myths and media manipulation were factors in how the war was viewed.

Jeremy Isaacs and Taylor Downing, *Cold War: An Illustrated History 1945–1991*. Boston: Little, Brown, 1998. Readable text with many photos and other illustrations. Presents clear, though limited, discussion of Vietnam.

David W. Levy, *The Debate over Vietnam*. Baltimore, MD: Johns Hopkins University Press, 1995. Well-written book focusing on American public opinion and how it shaped the war.

Frederik Logevall, *Choosing War: The Lost Chance for Peace and the Escalation of War in Vietnam*. Berkeley: University of California Press, 1999. An analysis of decision making during the critical period between 1963 and 1965.

Robert Mann, *A Grand Delusion: America's Descent into Vietnam*. New York: Basic Books, 2001. Lengthy and thorough history of the leaders and political environment that shaped American involvement in the war.

Ron Robin, *The Making of the Cold War Enemy*. Princeton, NJ: Princeton University Press, 2001. An analysis of how the United States used military leaders and scholars to predict enemy behavior and how their cultural biases affected their work.

Marilyn B. Young, *The Vietnam Wars, 1945–1990.* New York: HarperPerennial, 1990. Highly acclaimed, thorough history of both French and U.S. wars in Vietnam.

Qiang Zhai, *China and the Vietnam Wars, 1950–1975.* Chapel Hill: University of North Carolina Press, 2000. The first comprehensive investigation of China's foreign policy toward Vietnam, using archives not previously available.

Index

Picture Credits

Cover: Hulton Archive by Getty Images
Associated Press/AP Photo, 29, 44, 47, 49, 63, 71
© Bettmann/CORBIS, 9, 21, 26, 33, 35, 40, 41, 53, 57, 58, 60, 67, 68, 73, 74, 75, 80, 89
© CHAVUEL/DIEN BEIN PHU/CORBIS SYGMA, 31
© CORBIS, 54
Hulton Archive by Getty Images, 10, 14, 17, 36, 83, 86, 90
Steve Zmina, 18,30

About the Author

Laurel Corona lives in Lake Arrowhead, California, and teaches English and humanities at San Diego City College. She has a master's degree from the University of Chicago and a Ph.D. from the University of California at Davis. Dr. Corona has written may other books for Lucent Books, including *Afghanistan*, *Judaism*, *Life in Moscow*, *Peru*, and *The World Trade Center*.